# The World of Water

# Literature Bridges to Science Series

*The World of Water: Linking Fiction to Nonfiction.* By Phyllis J. Perry. 1995.

# The World of Water

## Linking Fiction to Nonfiction

PHYLLIS J. PERRY

TEACHER IDEAS PRESS
A Division of
Libraries Unlimited, Inc.
Englewood, Colorado
1995

TEACHER IDEAS PRESS
A Division of
Libraries Unlimited, Inc.
P.O. Box 6633
Englewood, CO 80155-6633
1-800-237-6124

Previously published as:

❄ *Bridges to the World of Water: Grades 5-9* ❄

**Library of Congress Cataloging-in-Publication Data**

Perry, Phyllis Jean.
    The world of water : linking fiction to nonfiction / Phyllis J. Perry.
    xvi, 149 p. 22x28 cm. -- (Literature bridges to science)
    Includes bibliographical references and index.
    ISBN 1-56308-321-3
    1. Water--Juvenile literature--Bibliography.  2. Water--Juvenile
fiction--Bibliography.  3. Children--Books and reading.  I. Title.
II. Series.
Z6004.H9P47      1995
[GB665]
551.46'0071'2--dc20                                      94-44426
                                                              CIP

For
Mother,
who loved the sea and singing about the *Titanic*,
and for
William, David, Stan, Jim, and Bobby,
who rescued me from the watery world.

# CONTENTS

# Part II
## Animals and Plants Living in and Around the Sea

# Part III
## Understanding, Exploring, and Surviving

## Part IV
## Environmental Concerns

# Part IV
## Environmental Concerns
### (*continued*)

📖 **NONFICTION CONNECTIONS** (*continued*)

# Part V
## Additional Resources and Linkages

# *About the Series*

In the era of literature-based reading programs, students are involved in narrative plots more than ever before, but they still face difficulty when confronted with expository text. Many experts believe that one of the best ways to teach anything is to *engage* the learner, that is, to get the student interested enough in a topic that the motivation to learn increases.

The Literature Bridges to Science series seeks to use the power of fictional works to bring students from the world of imagination into the world of the factual. In this series, fiction is used to build interest, increase familiarity with a topic, enlarge background, and introduce vocabulary. The fiction is to be enjoyed, letting the power of the story create a desire to learn more about a topic. Several fictional works are used; this suits individual tastes and the spread of experience in a group of students.

As student interest builds naturally, one "bridge" title (book, video, or other media) is then used to pique interest in a topical exploration. At this point, the teacher(s) can introduce a main theme or themes of study to the class, being confident that the learners are not starting at ground zero in their background knowledge of that topic. Interest in the topic might then be high enough to motivate the learners to attack the expository writing in nonfiction works.

Just as several fictional works are used to introduce a topic, the Literature Bridges to Science series suggests that numerous nonfiction works be offered to students as they begin their topical explorations. Thus, the series is particularly useful to those teachers who are transforming their teaching style from "sage on the stage" to *"guide* on the side." Nonfiction titles are chosen carefully to represent the more literary treatments of a topic in contrast to the boring exposition of a textbook-like stream of facts.

# *Introduction to the Book*

This book is designed to assist any busy teacher who is planning a middle-grade integrated unit of study involving oceans, rivers, and lakes. It includes suggestions for individual, small-group, and large-group activities across the disciplines. The multiple titles allow for student choice based on interests and skill levels. The titles were selected from a large number of books recommended by children's librarians with special expertise in books for young adults.

Between the fiction and nonfiction books in each section is a book or video that is suggested to serve as a "bridge." These bridges are books or films that combine factual information with fiction and enable the reader to make an easy transition from one type of material to another. *Night Dive* by Ann McGovern, *Sevengill, the Shark and Me* by Don Reed, and *Window on the Deep* by Andrea Conley are true-life adventures presented in a storylike format. *Free Willy* provides an opportunity to use a contemporary video to examine the complex relationships between humans and captive ocean creatures.

In parts I, II, III, and IV are detailed summaries of fiction books with discussion starters for each book, summaries of related nonfiction books of various lengths and levels of difficulty, and ideas for multidisciplinary activities arising out of the fiction and nonfiction books. The suggested activities involve skills in research, oral and written language, science, math, geography, and the arts. Each part begins with a "bookweb" suggesting a variety of ideas for discussion and projects that might come out of the fiction, nonfiction, and bridging materials. All suggested books have been published after 1980 and are easily available.

## 📖 Teaching Methods 📖

This book is designed to be used in a variety of teaching situations.

### One Teacher with Multiple Teaching Responsibilities

In some cases, a single teacher will be responsible for teaching a variety of subjects to a group of students. If the same teacher is responsible for teaching language arts, social studies, and science, this book—with its multidisciplining approach—will have a unifying effect on the curriculum.

The teacher might, for example, read aloud one of the fiction books in class before beginning this unit on the world of water. This will help set the tone for the study to come. As they hear a good piece of literature dealing with some aspect of the watery world, students will begin to think with new vocabulary, and to focus on ships, diving expeditions, creatures that live in the ocean and on its beaches, and freshwater fowl.

The teacher might suggest that students be alert to information in the mass media about oceans, rivers, and lakes. Encourage students to bring in articles from newspapers and magazines, which could be used to create a classroom vertical file. Alert the class (or have students alert their classmates) to opportunities for viewing television specials that might focus on some aspect of the watery world.

When this unit of study begins, the teacher might have each student select and read one of the fiction titles in part I. Afterward, encourage small-group discussions and sharing among those who have read the same book. This will extend reading, listening, and oral-language skills.

For the bridge book or video, the teacher might want to work with the class as a whole, assisting students who are not as comfortable with nonfiction as they are with fiction. Because the bridge combines elements of a story or real-life adventure with information and facts, students will be assisted in their transition from one type of reading to the other. Their growing vocabulary and knowledge of the watery world will be assets for learning to appreciate nonfiction.

As a composition activity, the teacher might assign writing topics that deal with the watery world. This might be combined with a science assignment. A student studying acid rain, for example, would have to do library research, learn appropriate procedures for footnoting and preparing a bibliography, and practice the elements of writing a persuasive essay.

As a creative-writing activity, have students, for example, write a piece of original dialog between two characters found in one of the literature books. Or, introduce poetry that is related to oceans, rivers, and lakes—and the birds and animals that live in such environments. Have students read nature poems and experiment with writing of their own.

Depending upon the books selected for this unit, history and geography might be combined in an activity where students trace the voyage of Charlotte Doyle or the ocean routes that various treasure-laden ships sailed.

## Departmentalization with Team Planning

In those schools where there is departmentalization with team planning time, language arts, social studies, and science teachers can plan a segment of time for a unit on the watery world.

The language arts teacher might create reading, research, and writing assignments that center around the fiction and the nonfiction books in this unit. Panel discussions and oral presentations of material will further speaking and listening skills. Specific skills such as skimming, reading for information, note taking, outlining, and using an index or a glossary of terms might also be introduced or reinforced using the suggested nonfiction books.

The social studies teacher might use this unit to discuss ocean exploration, famous voyages, or trade routes. This is a good time to concentrate on map-reading skills, making maps and using legends, computing distances on maps, and so on.

The science teacher might discuss orienteering and learning how to use a compass, charting a course across water, understanding navigation instruments such as the sextant and barometer, or the effects of oil spills and water pollution. This might be the time to set up a saltwater aquarium or to arrange a field trip to study pond life.

Some students will find it easy to take in the information that is presented as pictures or as graphs and charts in the nonfiction books. For other students, these will be new sources of information. Explain how to "read" these special materials, and create assignments that involve students in constructing tables and graphs.

Specialist teachers might also be involved in this unit. The music teacher might present sailor chanteys or recordings of whales. The art teacher might have students make ocean mobiles, collages of tissue-paper tropical fish, or clay models of ocean creatures. Arrange for classroom and hallway bulletin boards to feature ocean-related topics.

If the school has a computer lab, introduce students to software that deals with *The Voyage of the Mimi* (PBS series) or other video projects about the ocean, food chains, orienteering, treasure hunting, and so on. Have students use word-processing programs for reports related to this unit of study.

If the media specialist is the one responsible for teaching research skills to students, the classroom teacher might create activities that focus on topics that can be researched in CD encyclopedias (e.g., whales), vertical files on creatures that live in the sea, or computer databases (e.g., commercial fishing). Or, have the media specialist highlight those magazines and books in the collection that deal with the watery world, or even do some interlibrary loan to increase the materials available during this unit.

## Team Teaching

In those schools where team teaching occurs, the various team members might opt to present their favorite lessons and experiments. Choices might be based on personal expertise or interest in a new topic. Next, teachers might map out a sequence and timeline for their students that shows the connections between various subject areas.

While one teacher is presenting a lesson, colleagues might assist by leading small-group discussions, providing assistance for science experiments, or supervising small-group or individual research in the media center.

Some activities in a team teaching situation can be presented to a large group of students, such as films or videos. After the large-group presentation, team members might create and lead related small-group activities that give students opportunities to extend their knowledge.

## 📖 Culminating Activities 📖

Whatever the configuration of students and teachers, there might well be an opportunity for a special culminating activity for each part of this unit of study.

As a culminating activity for part I, which deals with ships, diving, and treasure, present students with a hypothetical scenario. For example: A group of treasure hunters has come upon a rich find in a sunken Spanish galleon off the coast of Florida. Who is entitled to the treasure? The individuals, the state of Florida, or the U.S. government? Or would it be divided? Have students research the current laws governing treasure. Have them estimate the cost and time to recover the treasure. Have them debate the merits of laws governing treasure finds.

As another culminating activity for part I, have students forecast the future. Will the time come when treasure hunters go to the moon or other planets in search of "treasure"? Have students compare and contrast deep-sea treasure hunting and deep-space treasure hunting.

As an example culminating activity for part IV, which deals with environmental concerns, have students suggest tangible ways for supporting an environmental conservation activity. Arrange for a supervised clean-up day along a local creek, or a student fund-raiser to support a special environmental group.

## 📖 Scope and Sequence 📖

Part I links ships, diving, and treasure. The literature books include contemporary fiction, fantasy, and historical fiction. Each book deals with some aspect of sailing and involves a treasure hunt or quest. The nonfiction books are also related to sailing, diving, sunken ships, and treasure hunting.

Part II links animals and plants living in and around the sea. The literature books include contemporary fiction and fantasy. The nonfiction books are related to various creatures and plants that live in oceans, rivers, and lakes.

Part III links understanding, exploring, and surviving in connection with oceans, rivers, and lakes. The literature books include survival stories, adventure, and fantasy. The nonfiction books provide information to help the student in understanding oceans, currents, waves, tides, and the land beneath the sea.

Part IV links environmental concerns. Each of the fiction books has a theme involving an endangered species, respect for wildlife, and the effects of greed and pollution on waters and the plants and creatures in them. Included are contemporary fiction and fantasy. The nonfiction books discuss such topics as endangered species, water pollution, and acid rain.

Part V is made up of additional resources and linkages. Included are questions that link various fiction books with one another; some additional suggestions for individual, small-group, and large-group activities; and ideas for using picture books with middle-grade readers. This section concludes with listings of other fiction books, nonfiction books, and selected magazines and videos that might be used in the classroom.

# Part I
# Ships, Diving, and Treasure

# Ships, Diving, and Treasure

## ◆ Literature Books ◆

📖*Beyond the Reef*
Chris moves to Florida and learns
to dive for treasure

📖*Dragon's Plunder*
Pirates and more pirates, for fantasy lovers

📖*The Last Voyage of the Misty Day*
Denny's adventures on an island
off the coast of Maine

📖*Stormsearch*
A mystery with a touch of history
on the coast of England

📖*The True Confessions of Charlotte Doyle*
The adventures of 13-year-old Charlotte
as she crosses the Atlantic in 1832

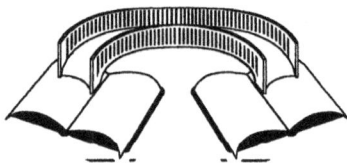

## ◆ Bridge ◆

📖*Night Dive*
Adventures while scuba
diving at night on a coral
reef

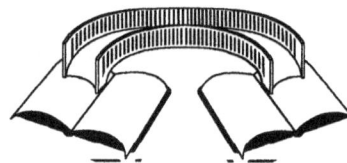

## ◆ Nonfiction Connections ◆

📖*Diving for Treasure*
For serious divers only

📖*Diving to the Past: Recovering
Ancient Wrecks*
Salvaging ancient wrecks with
conservational concern

📖*Footsteps in the Ocean: Careers in
Diving*
Diving for sport and business

📖*The Lost Wreck of the Isis*
The JASON project and its deep-
sea discoveries

📖*Mysteries of the Deep*
A challenging book of sunken
treasures, mysterious voyages,
strange creatures, and unexplained disappearances

📖*Shipwrecks: Terror and Treasure*
Three famous shipwrecks, and the
dives to photograph and recover
their treasures

📖*Sunken Ships & Treasure*
Famous shipwrecks and treasure
hunts

### OTHER TOPICS TO EXPLORE

—Lighthouses
—Doctors who dive
—Salvage
—Propulsion
—Privateers

—Types of sailing vessels
—Ship models
—Wrecks on shipping lanes
—Recovering ancient wrecks
—Underwater photography

—Sonar
—The Bermuda Triangle
—Maritime museums
—Ship graveyards
—Spanish galleons

From *Bridges to the World of Water*. © 1995. Teacher Ideas Press. (800) 237-6124.

# 📖 *Literature Books* 📖

## Ships, Diving, and Treasure

---

### ◆ Literature Books ◆

📖*Beyond the Reef*
Chris moves to Florida and learns to dive for treasure

📖*Dragon's Plunder*
Pirates and more pirates, for fantasy lovers

📖*The Last Voyage of the Misty Day*
Denny's adventures on an island off the coast of Maine

📖*Stormsearch*
A mystery with a touch of history on the coast of England

📖*The True Confessions of Charlotte Doyle*
The adventures of 13-year-old Charlotte as she crosses the Atlantic in 1832

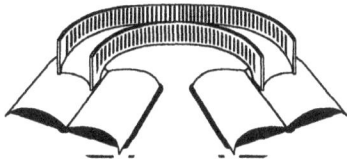

---

### ◆ Bridge ◆

📖*Night Dive*
Adventures while scuba diving at night on a coral reef

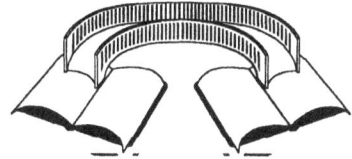

---

### ◆ Nonfiction Connections ◆

📖*Diving for Treasure*
For serious divers only

📖*Diving to the Past: Recovering Ancient Wrecks*
Salvaging ancient wrecks with conservational concern

📖*Footsteps in the Ocean: Careers in Diving*
Diving for sport and business

📖*The Lost Wreck of the Isis*
The JASON project and its deep-sea discoveries

📖*Mysteries of the Deep*
A challenging book of sunken treasures, mysterious voyages, strange creatures, and unexplained disappearances

📖*Shipwrecks: Terror and Treasure*
Three famous shipwrecks, and the dives to photograph and recover their treasures

📖*Sunken Ships & Treasure*
Famous shipwrecks and treasure hunts

#### OTHER TOPICS TO EXPLORE

| | | |
|---|---|---|
| —Lighthouses | —Types of sailing vessels | —Sonar |
| —Doctors who dive | —Ship models | —The Bermuda Triangle |
| —Salvage | —Wrecks on shipping lanes | —Maritime museums |
| —Propulsion | —Recovering ancient wrecks | —Ship graveyards |
| —Privateers | —Underwater photography | —Spanish galleons |

# 📖 *Beyond the Reef*

by Todd Strasser

New York: Bantam Doubleday Dell, 1989. 243p.

---

### Type of Book:

This is a realistic, contemporary story told in the first person from the viewpoint of a seventeen-year-old boy.

### Setting:

Key West, Florida.

### Major Characters:

Chris Cooper and his mother and father; Chris's schoolmates Shannon Horn, Billy Peebles, and David Lester; Shannon's mother, Betty; Tom, a fishing guide who becomes a family friend; and Bobby Clark, a college sophomore who comes to Florida to dive with them.

### Other Books by the Author:

*The Accident* (New York: Delacorte Press, 1988), *The Complete Computer Popularity Program* (New York: Dell, 1984), and *The Diving Bell* (New York: Scholastic, 1992).

## —PLOT SUMMARY—

As the book opens, Chris is reflecting on his simple life of five years ago when he and his family lived in New York, where his dad was a teacher and his mother wrote for the local newspaper. Chris traces his current circumstances back to an Easter trip when his family vacationed in Key West and his father accidentally witnessed a find by treasure divers.

Chris's parents decide to move to Key West, where Mom will write her novel and Dad will look for treasure. In August, they return to Key West and rent a very small house. Dad buys an old boat, the *Treasure Hunter*. Mom begins to do some writing. Chris helps on the boat and also makes friends with a twelve-year-old girl, Shannon, who lives next door.

After a few months, Chris feels at home. But his mom has nothing to do except watch TV, and although his dad keeps looking for treasure, he finds nothing of value. Dad begins to look like a bum. There are arguments and tension between Chris's parents.

Some folks make fun of Chris's dad. There are acts of vandalism. Money is scarce, so Mom takes a job as a waitress five nights a week at a fancy restaurant called the Pier House. This gets them through the school year and the next summer.

In their second fall at Key West, Dad comes home with his first real treasure, a bunch of silver coins fused together. Dad cleans and separates the silver coins and sells them. He also cuts his hair and cleans up his appearance.

Instead of spending treasure money on home improvements, Dad buys an air compressor and other diving equipment. To avoid hearing his mom and dad fight, Chris goes to Shannon's house, where Shannon's mother, Betty, offers to pay him $3 a piece for shark teeth, which she uses in her jewelry making.

At school, Chris deals with the locals (conches), who dislike strangers. A bully named Billy Peebles, who is a conch, makes trouble for Chris. After school,

4

Chris borrows Shannon's skiff and catches a small shark. Then something hits the boat, knocking Chris into the water. He manages to climb back in before the boat whizzes off with something pulling it.

Chris is pulled into the Gulf of Mexico by a great white shark. When the line finally goes limp, Chris begins to row for home. A trawler finds him, and when Dad and Tom reach Chris, the head of a 2,000-pound shark is still attached to the line. Chris sells the teeth to Betty for $129.

The following summer, Chris and Shannon dive to help Dad find treasure, and they discover an anchor. All three are diving when they are caught in a squall. Shannon's hair gets caught underwater in the port drive shaft, and she is struck by the hull of the boat. Chris saves her life by cutting her hair and pulling her back up to the surface.

For the next six weeks, they dive and find a lot of artifacts. Bobby Clark, a sophomore in college, comes to join them. On his first day out, Bobby finds a small gold bar. They also find some gold coins and a gold cup. Some of the school kids stop by the celebration party that night.

Dad goes to Miami with the treasure and comes back with presents and a State of Florida Admiralty Injunction giving him the exclusive right to search for treasure in the scatter pattern. He has also bought the *Dolphin*, a sixty-five-foot Coast Guard cutter that's in terrible shape.

Chris is now called "the treasure hunter's kid" instead of "snowbird," a term for a visitor or newcomer from up north. Bobby Clark decides to stay out of college and continue to dive. Bobby is made captain of the boat, and he hires five other divers. Although they keep finding things like gold rings and chains, they are always short of money.

Chris decides to try his hand at catching jumbo shrimp, thinking the money will help. Shannon tries to discourage him because the railroad bridge where the shrimping occurs is for conches only. On the bridge, Chris gets in a fight with Billy.

By summer, Dad is out of money. Chris's grandmother has a heart attack, and his mom tells Chris she is flying home

to see her and won't be coming back. Grandmother survives, and Mom gets her old job back in Flintville. Chris visits at Christmas but, in spite of exciting activities, decides to return to Key West.

Dad tries to interest Miami investors in his treasure hunting. His presentation goes well until it is contested by a man from "Stop 'Em," a group that tries to protect elderly investors. When the evening ends, not a single share has been sold. Dad decides that he and Chris will go to Spain to do some research about sunken treasure ships.

In Spain, Chris does schoolwork and Dad spends every day in the Archivo General de Indias, where he studies sheets of old paper, *legajos*, and finally comes upon information about a ship called the *Sevilla* that set sail in 1632 and was captured by the Dutch off the coast of Florida.

Using a code from the anchor they found, Dad learns that this anchor was from the *Sevilla*'s sister ship, the *Flora*. Chris helps his father in reading the *legajos*. They also hire a young scholar, Julios, to help them research.

Chris decides to return to Flintville after Christmas, while Dad remains in Spain. But just before Christmas, Chris finds *Los Papeles de Juan Ferrer*, the writings of a seventeen-year-old who had sailed on the *Flora*. In it, Chris reads the account of the sinking of the treasure galleon *Sevilla*.

With this information, Dad and Chris return to Key West. Chris, Shannon, Bobby, and his friend Tammi go out in the *Dolphin*. They have a close encounter with a hammerhead shark.

Mom visits but returns to Flintville, and Dad interests new investors in his treasure hunting. Diving begins again. The *Treasure Hunter* has been overhauled and is back in the water. They finally have a successful dive, finding a six-foot-square area covered with 850 gold coins. The press surround them with publicity.

Chris's classmate David invites Chris and Shannon to have dinner at his house. Chris's dad is away on business. That night at home, Chris feels uneasy. He calls his mom in Flintville, but she isn't home.

Chris is hit over the head by an intruder and wakes up in the hospital.

He learns that someone broke into the house, perhaps to steal treasure. The intruder left the gas jet turned on in the oven. If Shannon, alerted by a call from Chris's mom, had not come over and found him, Chris would have died. As it is, he only has a concussion and will be able to dive again in two weeks.

Chris's mom flies down to Key West. She's furious that he was home alone and wants to take him back to Flintville. Dad returns and says things will change. Mom agrees to stay for a few days, and they move to a tourist resort, Coral Lodge, where they stay free in exchange for letting the Lodge display some of the treasures.

Mom again returns to Flintville. As soon as school is out, Chris begins diving. No more treasure is found and, because they have no money, Chris and his dad have to move out of their Coral Lodge bungalow. This time they go to live on an old, broken-down sailboat.

Things continue to go badly. The *Treasure Hunter* is back in dry dock. Chris's dad and the crew decide to spend two weeks diving outside the reef thinking the galleon *Sevilla* may have sunk there. While searching, Chris gets up early to start the bilge pump, and finds that the *Dolphin* is listing. It suddenly rolls over, trapping Chris inside.

Chris opens the escape hatch but is so weak he can't swim out. Shannon rescues Chris, but Bobby is found dead. The *Dolphin* sinks, and they return to land on a trawler. Bobby's brother takes Bobby home for burial.

Dad now has almost given up hope of finding the treasure. He's lost the *Dolphin* and its special equipment, and the *Treasure Hunter* is still in dry dock. Dad doesn't eat or shower often. There's no money. Chris finally confronts his dad about his drinking and about not diving.

Chris tries to come up with a way to make money for expenses. First, he thinks he'll do magic tricks for tourists in the square. Instead, David and Shannon invite him to help net shrimp from the bridge. They haul in 120 pounds. Even Billy Peebles adds a bucket to their catch.

The next morning, Chris finds an envelope of money and knows it is more than his share of the shrimp haul. Dad learns Peebles Salvage brought up the equipment from the *Dolphin* and put it on the *Treasure Hunter,* which has been overhauled and is out of dry dock.

The summer before Chris's senior year, Chris and his dad dive again outside the reef. They find a few artifacts. School starts. Chris applies himself to his studies and starts looking at colleges. Dad finds some cannons, takes pictures, and, on the basis of the photos, gets another loan. He moves them into a decent house.

In May, Chris dives and discovers a strange "bump" beneath the sea that turns out to be a pile of gold five feet high. At last, he has found the treasure of the *Sevilla*. The investors and divers are paid. Shannon has enough money to go to college. Money is also sent to Bobby's family. Dad even donates a cannon and some artifacts to the town for display.

Mom and Dad now can afford to keep a house in Flintville and another in Key West. Mom begins writing a novel. Dad uses his new diving ship, the *Bobby Clark,* to search for the wreck of a galleon off the coast of Costa Rica.

Chris enrolls at a small college and Shannon at a large university about sixty miles away. They see each other on weekends, and in the summer continue to dive with Chris's father.

## 📖 Discussion Starters 📖

*Beyond the Reef*
by Todd Strasser

**1** Before Chris moves to Florida, he visits the state. One of the first things he does there is buy a shark's tooth. Shark teeth then play two more major roles in the book. In what ways are shark teeth used again, and how does this recurring theme function in the book?

**2** There are the "conches" and the "snowbirds" in this story. Are these good labels for the "natives" and the "visitors" (or "newcomers")? Why or why not? Can you think of other similar words that are used in other parts of the country to describe people?

**3** Diving for treasure sounds glamorous and exciting. But in this book, you learn that it takes not only luck, but knowledge, years of hard work, and the investment of a lot of money to locate treasure. Do you think you'd like to be a deep-sea treasure hunter? Why or why not?

**4** *Los Papeles de Juan Ferrer* is a factual account of sailing. Mom begins to write fiction in the beginning of this book but soon gives up. At the end of the book, she is writing again and this time her story line appears to be based on the real-life struggles of her own family. Do you think it would be easier to write a novel that was entirely fictional or one that was based on true adventures? Why?

**5** This book chronicles the tension between "newcomers" and "old-timers" in a town. This same tension can be felt when someone tries to enter any new group. Have you ever had the feeling of being an "outsider" when you tried to join a group? What causes these feelings? What did you do to try to gain acceptance into a new group? Did it work?

**6** The overall story line in this book wouldn't be much different if Chris had never had his adventure with the great white shark in chapter 7. Why do you think this chapter is included in the book? Does it have a special function?

**7** Chris and Shannon each save the other's life during the course of this book. Have you read other stories where one character saves the life of another? Do you think that saving the life of another establishes a special bond? Why or why not?

**8** Chris's mom thinks that her husband is almost obsessed with treasure hunting. She points out that her husband's parents were obsessed with gambling. Some people like to bet on the outcome of games or horse races. Some like to gamble at slot machines or in casinos. The *Treasure Hunter* itself, like a horse, is a sort of gamble. How would you distinguish between someone who likes to gamble now and then and someone who is addicted to gambling?

**9** Billy Peebles changes from being a totally obnoxious conch to being a helpful friend to Chris by the end of the story. Why do you think Billy changes his attitude?

**10** Many mysterious incidents happen throughout the book that remain unexplained at the end of the story. Who puts sugar in the gas tank? Who renames the *Treasure Hunter*? Who hits Chris over the head? Is the oven gas jet in Chris's house left on by accident or on purpose after Chris is hit? What is your explanation for each of these events?

From *Bridges to the World of Water*. © 1995. Teacher Ideas Press. (800) 237-6124.

## 📖 Multidisciplinary Activities 📖

*Beyond the Reef*
by Todd Strasser

**1** Chris and his family move to Key West, Florida, from Flintville, New York. Use a road map to route the shortest driving trip from New York City to Key West. How many miles is it? If you estimate 30 miles to a gallon of gas and $1.35 per gallon, how much will the fuel cost to make the trip by car? If you drive an average of 55 miles an hour for eight hours each day, how long will it take to make the trip?

**2** Florida is often called "The Sunshine State." Do some research. How many sunny days does Florida average each year. What is the average daytime temperature in Florida during each month of the year? Find the same information for the state in which you live. (If you live anywhere in Florida, pick another state where a relative of yours lives to make the comparison.) Make a graph comparing the state in which you live to Florida, based on the number of sunny days each year and the average daytime temperature during each month of the year. Share it with your class.

**3** There is an organization mentioned in this book that is dedicated to making sure that elderly investors don't lose their money in a scam. What organizations exist to provide information and protection to senior citizens? What are some benefits to belonging to these organizations? If there are representatives of any of these groups in your community, interview one in person or by telephone. Prepare questions ahead of time. Share what you learn with your class.

From *Bridges to the World of Water.* © 1995. Teacher Ideas Press. (800) 237-6124.

# 📖 *Dragon's Plunder*

by Brad Strickland
New York: Atheneum, 1992. 153p.

**Type of Book:**
This is a fantasy written in the form of a pirate adventure story.

**Setting:**
Most of the action of the story takes place on the brig, on the *Bouncing Betty Bowers*, or on Windrose Island.

**Major Characters:**
Jamie Falconer, a fifteen-year-old orphan; Captain Octavius Deadmon; Mr. Andrew Pye, the first mate; the parrot Squok; the Princess Amelia of Laurel; Mrs. Clara Llewellen, her governess; and Gravis the Gray, a dragon.

**Other Books by the Author:**
*Moon Dreams* (New York: New American Library, 1988), *Nul's Quest* (New York: New American Library, 1989), and *Shadowshow* (New York: New American Library, 1988).

## —PLOT SUMMARY—

The story opens in the inn where Jamie works. A stranger gives him a silver coin and asks him to fetch the innkeeper, Mr. Growdy. Then the stranger gives the innkeeper a golden coin to pay in advance for the expenses of eight men who'll be spending a week at the inn while their ship the *Bouncing Betty Bowers* is loaded with provisions and undergoes light repairs.

The first mate, Mr. Andrew Pye, explains that they are privateers working under a fifty-one-year-old commission from King Carleton II for operations against the Zamps and Vrenkons. The captain of his ship is Captain Octavius Deadmon.

When Mr. Growdy wonders why disreputable people like privateers stay at his inn, Jamie suggests that it is due to the sign outside. The sign painter misinterpreted the instructions and painted Pirate's Rest as the name for the inn instead of Parrot's Roost.

Just leaving the inn that afternoon by coach is one of the west country's many princesses, Amelia, with her governess, Mrs. Llewellen. The princess, who is fifteen, wishes they could stay to meet the pirates, but her governess says their grand tour is over and they must return home.

The eight officers from the ship *Betty* arrive at the inn that night. Captain Deadmon, however, does not come because he is staying on the ship to oversee the repairs. Other seamen have found less expensive lodgings in the town. More than once, Mr. Pye tries to explain to the innkeeper that they are not pirates but privateers. As Jamie listens to them, he longs to go to sea and escape the drudgery of life at the inn.

The innkeeper wants the men to leave as soon as possible because they eat so much food. He takes Jamie outside and bids him to use his magic to whistle up a good east wind so that the privateers will be on their way. Jamie does not want to do this because working magic makes his head ache, but he does as he is asked. (It is explained that one in ten people have a magic gift, but most of their magic is useless. Jamie is thought to be lucky to have such a useful talent.)

The next morning, Jamie awakes to strange sounds. Before he can investigate, he is kidnapped. He convinces the sailors to take the gag out of his mouth and then tells them that he really wants to join their crew. He is allowed to make a brief trip back to the inn to get his few things and to pick up Squok, his parrot.

Once on board the ship, Jamie is taken to a small compartment and told to rest there. When he awakens the next morning, Jamie and Squok look about the boat. Jamie is invited to have breakfast with Mr. Pye and meet the captain afterward to sign on as a crew member.

As soon as Squok sees Captain Deadmon, he leaps onto his shoulder. The Captain recognizes him as a parrot he lost thirty years before. The Captain is a strange-looking man, and he and Mr. Pye tell Jamie an unusual story. The Captain was once a pirate. When he was only twenty-four years old, he swore an oath that he would never rest until he had taken a dragon's hoard as a prize. Twenty years ago, the Captain was killed, but his spirit cannot rest until he fulfills his oath. And each year, the Captain has fewer and fewer of his original, faithful crew to help him.

They have tried to find a dragon, to take its treasure, and fulfill the Captain's oath, but so far they have failed. They have heard, however, that a dragon still lives on Windrose Island. They have tried to reach this spot, but there is never a favorable wind to blow them there. It is the Captain's hope that Jamie can whistle up a wind for them.

Jamie signs on as cabin boy, and Squok stays with him and agrees to help train him in the ways of the ship. Jamie also has to take lessons from Mr. Pye and other members of the ship's crew in various scholarly subjects. Before they set off on their long voyage, Jamie, Mr. Pye, and two crewmen, Sharkey and Wicks, go to Pridden Town to buy some necessities for Jamie.

The town is shut up and quiet. Something is wrong. Suddenly Mr. Pye and the others are set upon by townspeople who incorrectly believe they are pirates from Roger Hawke's ship, the *Flying Terror*, which attacked their town just yesterday. Hawke is an old enemy of Captain Deadmon.

Mr. Pye buys Jamie clothes, and then they hurry back with their news to the *Betty*. Before they reach the *Betty*, however, Hawke's ship, the *Flying Terror* appears and fires a cannon at them. Jamie whistles up a wind to allow the *Betty* to escape, but the wind swamps the small boat he, Mr. Pye, and the two crewmen are in. Jamie and his friends are captured and taken aboard the *Flying Terror*. They pretend to be from the town, and they are held captive on board in hopes that someone from the town may ransom them.

The four men from the Betty are chained in the bottom of the *Flying Terror*. When one of the guards goes up for some rum, they manage to work their chains free, but each of the men remains handcuffed to another. Mr. Pye is chained to Jamie, and Sharkey is handcuffed to Wicks.

Later, they trick the guard into leaving, escape from the hold, and plot to blow a hole in the ship. After they have located the gunpowder and left a short candle to burn down and cause an explosion, Squok, the parrot, appears to tell them he's come to help. He knows where the *Betty* is waiting.

Squok imitates the captain and tricks a crewman into giving them the keys to free the four crewmen from the *Betty*. The powder explodes, and there is wild confusion on the ship. Mr. Pye and Jamie rescue two other prisoners on board, who turn out to be the young princess Amelia and her companion, Mrs. Llewellen, from the inn. The four crewmen from the *Betty* and the two rescued females escape from the sinking ship in a small boat.

Crewmen from the *Flying Terror* fire at them, but the *Betty* comes into sight and fires back at the *Flying Terror*, which sinks. The *Betty* then picks up its four crew members as well as Amelia and Mrs. Llewellen. Five small lifeboats from the *Flying Terror* escape, and crew members threaten to return with Hawke.

Captain Deadmon explains that he cannot take Amelia and Mrs. Llewellen home because Hawke stands in their way. They agree to stay on the *Betty* as it sets off to find the home of the dragon. Mr. Pye gives up his cabin to the women. Amelia begins to dress as a boy, and she tells Jamie all about her very modest kingdom as she joins him in his school lessons.

When they finally come within sight of Windrose Island, where a dragon is supposed to live, the captain sends Squok to look around for them. Jamie tries to whistle up a wind to take them in, but he fails, for another wind is working against him. Mrs. Llewellen suggests that she compose a tune and Mr. Pye write a song with strong words that Jamie can whistle. They do so and succeed.

When they are in safe harbor, all of the crew go ashore except for three men who stay to guard the women and the ship. Amelia, however, manages to sneak ashore with the others. All the men are armed except for Jamie. He takes a special pair of pistols that were on display in the great cabin of the *Betty*.

They make camp on shore and the next morning set off to find the dragon. When they reach the dragon's lair, Amelia slips inside and Jamie follows her. Inside, they find Gravis the Gray, a dragon who has an enormous collection of books. It turns out that Gravis has spent all of his gold and jewels on books. He is a philosopher.

While Jamie is talking with the dragon, the Captain, Mr. Pye, and others come in. Jamie learns that Hawke has used the same wind to follow the *Betty* and has captured her. One of Hawke's men has injured Mr. Pye. One of the crew members, a surgeon, stitches up Mr. Pye's cuts, and they plan what to do next.

The dragon explains that he does not want to fight but would help them if he could. Because he no longer has his fire breath, he has nothing with which to fight. The Captain sends Mr. Pye and Jamie to seek terms from Hawke, warning them to beware of possible treachery.

Hawke delivers his terms, which include leaving all of Captain Deadmon's men stranded on the island; taking the *Betty*, the two women, and the four men who helped to sink the *Flying Terror*; yielding up Captain Deadmon to be chopped to pieces; and giving up the head of the dragon and its treasure. Jamie and Mr. Pye return to the dragon's lair.

Captain Deadmon and his crew reject these terms and decide to fight. The dragon shows them another way out of the cave. The *Betty's* crew leave and sneak up on the pirates camped on the beach. They fight, but the odds are against them, and it appears that they will lose. Then Jamie starts to whistle. The wind fights with them, and Captain Deadmon's crew wins the day.

But before they can celebrate, Hawke's guns begin firing at them. The men on land can also see that Mrs. Llewellen is being held on the ship. Mr. Pye and Jamie set out in a small boat, but they are fired upon. They look up and see the dragon flying above them. Gravis vaporizes the shot that is aimed at him. He rescues Mrs. Llewellen and destroys the ship's cannon. Hawke's crew leap overboard in fear.

Mr. Pye takes over the ship and is soon joined by Captain Deadmon and the others. They learn that the dragon's rejuvenated fire breath is completely the work of the cook who brewed up two charges for the dragon to use. They find that this pirate ship is loaded with treasure. They also learn that the ship is called the *Golden Dragon*. The captain has finally succeeded in fulfilling his oath to capture a dragon's treasure.

The crew moves all the cargo from the *Betty* to the *Golden Dragon*. Mr. Pye asks Mrs. Llewellen to marry him. Captain Deadmon agrees to perform the ceremony. Mr. Pye, released from his duty, says that he and his new wife will retire from the sea to Great Camford, where he will publish books, including his own poetry and the philosophical writings of the dragon.

Princess Amelia suggests to Captain Deadmon that Jamie be made captain of the *Golden Dragon*. She says that Jamie can be an admiral in her navy. Captain Deadmon agrees to this, says good-bye, and returns to the now empty *Betty*.

Captain Deadmon sails off alone in the ship, and as he leaves, Gravis the Gray flies along with him. Those who are watching can see the ship ascend into the sky.

Squok has given Captain Deadmon his promise to remain with Jamie and help him learn what he needs to know. Jamie orders that the *Golden Dragon* be made ready and says that they will catch the morning tide to return home.

# 📖 Discussion Starters 📖

*Dragon's Plunder*
by Brad Strickland

**1** Much of what happens in this book could happen in any pirate or adventure story, but some of the elements could only take place in a *fantasy*. Identify at least four elements of the story that could only happen in a fantasy.

**2** Sometimes authors give their characters names that are singularly appropriate to the character. Study the names in this story. Are there some that seem to be especially appropriate? Which ones and why?

**3** There are only three illustrations in this book. Why do you think these were included? If you could have chosen the scenes to be illustrated, are these the three you would have picked? If not, which other scenes would you like to have seen illustrated and why?

**4** Squok has many important functions in the book. Review the story and name some of the specific things that Squok accomplishes that no other character in the book could.

**5** The cook, Barbecue Timson, seems to be only a comic character when he first appears, but it turns out that he has a very important role. What unique role does he play? When did you first suspect that he would be called upon to do something special? What made you think this?

**6** All the ships in the story have particularly interesting names. What was each ship called, and why do you think that its name was or was not a good one for it? If you were renaming these ships (which you can't do because it's bad luck!), what would you call them?

**7** The first mate, Mr. Pye, explains that his crew members are not pirates but privateers, because they hold a commission from the former king for operations against the Zamps and Vrenkons. The main battles in the book, however, are against a pirate, Hawke. Is there much distinction between a pirate and a privateer? If so, what is the difference, and why is it important?

**8** Most people hold a stereotype of a dragon in their mind. What elements make up that stereotype? Discuss all the ways in which Gravis the Gray does and does not fit the stereotype.

**9** It is pointed out that only one in ten of the people who inhabit this fantasy world have magic, and that of those who do have magic, very few have useful magic. If you were the author and were handing out one more magical ability to one of your characters, what additional magical ability would you give, and to which character would you give it? Why?

**10** Jamie and Amelia have to study lessons four or five hours a day while on the *Betty*. They study natural sciences, mathematics, astronomy, navigation, Vrenkish, elocution, composition, and literature. Once the daily routine of schooling is established, the topic is brought up only once again. When is schooling brought up again, and why is it brought up?

---

# 📖 Multidisciplinary Activities 📖

### *Dragon's Plunder*
### by Brad Strickland

**1** In this book, it is very important that there be a strong wind to blow the ship's occupants to the shore. Sometimes winds are helpful, but sometimes they are very destructive. Depending upon the strength of the wind and whether or not it contains moisture or has a circular activity, winds have names such as *gales*, *hurricanes*, *typhoons*, and *tornadoes*. Research winds that are particularly destructive. Report what you learn to your class.

**2** The distance that a ship travels is not measured in *miles*, and its speed is not measured in *miles per hour*. What forms of measurement are used? Can one system of measurement be converted to *miles* and *miles per hour*, such as car distance and speed to ship distance and speed? What is the top speed of a typical, modern ocean liner? How far is it from New York to Portsmouth, England? If a modern ocean liner did not stop, and if it kept a steady, top speed, how many hours would it need to travel from New York to Portsmouth, England?

**3** Mrs. Llewellen writes a tune to Mr. Pye's verse to make a strong song that will create a powerful wind. Write your own original sea chantey and share it with your class.

From *Bridges to the World of Water*. © 1995. Teacher Ideas Press. (800) 237-6124.

# 📖 *The Last Voyage of the Misty Day*

by Jackie French Koller
New York: Atheneum, 1992. 154p.

**Type of Book:**
  This is a contemporary story told in the third person from the viewpoint of Denny Townsend, a fourteen-year-old girl.

**Setting:**
  The story takes place at Phinney's Island on the coast of Maine.

**Major Characters:**
  Denny Townsend, age fourteen; her mother, Kathy; Mr. Jones, a retired engineer; Spence, a high school student; and Andrea Flemming, Mr. Jones's daughter.

**Other Books by the Author:**
  *If I Had One Wish* (Boston: Little, Brown, 1991), *Nothing to Fear* (San Diego, Calif.: Harcourt Brace Jovanovich, 1991), and *The Primrose Way* (New York: Harcourt Brace Jovanovich, 1992). Two of her short fantasy books are *A Dragon in the Family* (1993) and *The Dragonling* (1990), both published by Little, Brown.

## —PLOT SUMMARY—

Denny's mother, Kathy, visited the coast of Maine when she was young. So it is to Phinney's Island, off the Maine coast, that she comes from Brooklyn, New York, after the death of her husband. She brings along her fourteen-year-old daughter, Denny, who is most reluctant to leave behind her friends and a beautiful Brooklyn apartment to come to this isolated place.

Denny hates the way the kids talk and dress, and she has no friends in this new place. She refers to the local folk as "Mainiacs." Her mother is frequently in tears, still grieving for her husband. She's had to put her writing career on hold to look for a job to support Denny and herself.

From her house, Denny can see Little Hog Island. She notices a light there. There is an old story that a causeway used to connect the island. Now, only when the tide is low and the land is exposed can someone walk or drive to the island. The story also tells about Rufus Day, a hermit who lived on Little Hog Island, who refused to leave during a hurricane in 1954. His house blew away, and Rufus and his boat, the *Misty Day*, were never seen again. Twenty years later, the *Misty Day* reappeared, and a relative had it dragged back up onto Little Hog Island.

Kathy finds a job in the general store in Wellsley, a very small town consisting of the store, a Congregational church, and a barn that serves as a town hall, a fire station, and a police station.

When Denny sees smoke coming from Little Hog Island, she decides to go investigate what she thinks may be a ghost ship. Denny is trying to keep out of sight and to find the source of the smoke and a whining sound when she comes upon a sea captain on board the *Misty Day*. Before she can leave, an ugly pug dog, Marty, runs up and bites her sock.

The captain, a man of about seventy-five years, comes to investigate. He mistakes Denny for a boy and says that his name is Jones and that he is a retired engineer from Connecticut who lives on the boat. He explains that he drives back and forth between the mainland and the island when the tide is low.

When she hears about the captain, Denny's mother, Kathy, is suspicious, and goes out with Denny the next day to meet him. Mr. Jones shows them around the boat and says he'll work on the inside during the winter, spruce up the outside in the spring, and then it will be ready to sail again.

The next Saturday, Denny returns and pesters the captain until he agrees to let her stay and help him with the engines. On Sunday she comes again. She brings the captain some soup and manages to make friends with the dog. Denny learns that the captain's wife, Martha, died three years ago. Denny tells him about her father, and she also sees a picture of the captain's daughter, Andrea, who is a lawyer in New York.

Mr. Jones, bringing flowers from town, comes over and joins Denny and her mother for Thanksgiving. At this time, Denny's mother gives her a present. This is a tradition that always marked the beginning of the Christmas season when Denny's father, John, was alive. Reminded again of the death of her father, which seems so unfair to her, Denny becomes upset and throws the package into a picture, breaking the glass. While her mother is preparing the turkey, Mr. Jones takes Denny out to gather mussels, which they cook and add to the Thanksgiving feast.

They eat, and afterward Mr. Jones cleans out the blocked chimney. Mr. Jones encourages Denny to talk. She explains that each Christmas her father would buy a book for her and that, on Thanksgiving, they'd bring out and read the old Christmas books. Later that night, Denny unwraps the package her mother gave her earlier, the traditional advent calendar, and she hangs it up.

A nor'easter hits on Christmas Eve, and Kathy and Denny worry about Mr. Jones. But early on Christmas morning, Mr. Jones appears with presents. The power has gone out up and down the coast. He invites them to come to his boat where it's warm. His presents to them are ice shoes that he's made out of boards with nails in them. They use these to walk through the beautiful world of ice that the storm has left them.

Mr. Jones tells them how he met his wife, Martha, on VJ day, wrote to her every day, and married her a month later. In looking through old pictures, Denny comes upon a class picture of Mr. Jones's daughter, but she's listed as Andrea Flemming. When Denny asks about the different last name, Mr. Jones makes up an excuse about it being a school mistake.

As the winter continues, Kathy starts writing again, and Denny and Mr. Jones work on the boat engines. The port engine is named Penelope and the starboard engine is named Stella. Mr. Jones seems to have developed a limp but snaps at Denny when she notices and mentions it. In March, Mr. Jones buys a dinghy and comes to row her out when Denny toots on a portable air horn.

Mr. Jones hires Spence, a boy from high school that Denny particularly dislikes, to come and help with the engines. Mr. Jones explains that he needs to work more quickly and have the boat in the water by the end of June. Although she denies it, Denny begins to like Spence as they work together. Denny also decides it is time to let her hair grow out.

One day, Denny accidentally comes upon a book, Rufus Day's ship's log. The captain is furious when he sees her reading it. The next day, Mr. Jones apologizes and produces the book, with all the pages except the first illegible. Denny is not at all sure it is the same log she found the day before.

Denny has overheard some boys teasing Spence at school, saying he spends too much time on the boat. Spence tries to act tough and says he's only helping because the captain is rich. The boys think that Spence will one day relieve the captain of his bankroll. Worried about what she's heard, Denny relays this information to the captain. Mr. Jones simply says he'll keep a lookout but believes that Spence is okay.

At one point they almost lose the boat when a chain breaks and the boat starts down into the water. Denny's quick thinking, which leads to wedging a timber between the wall and the winch, saves the day, but the distributor breaks down before they can pull the boat back to safety. Denny proposes a rubber band as a temporary solution, and she saves the day again.

The next day, Spence sits next to Denny on the school bus. He is reading *The Red Badge of Courage*. Denny makes a remark that offends him, so Spence moves out of the seat. Denny writes a note of apology. When the bus stops, Spence gets out and walks her home. He says she's pretty with her long hair.

Denny's mother gets a call saying a publisher might want to publish her book. She'll be flying to New York for a day to discuss the contract. While her mother is off in New York, Denny hears a dog yapping, and she tries to raise Mr. Jones by using the air horn. Denny sees what looks like Spence's red boat. No one responds to her calls, so Denny decides to go over.

Denny can't swim and falls into the four-foot-deep water, but manages to get across. She sees the dog, Marty. He has a bloody eye and his front left paw is hurt. In the boat, Denny finds Mr. Jones, sprawled on the floor with a gash on his head.

Denny uses the ship-to-shore radio to call for help. The Coast Guard comes and takes Mr. Jones to the town of Machias. Denny stays behind to help the police. Because she's seen Spence's red boat, Denny is sure he is the one who has ransacked the cabin.

The police and Denny go to Spence's home, where his mother says he's been all evening. Spence explains that he loaned his boat to some boys to do night fishing, and he offers to take the police to them.

Spence and Denny go to the hospital to see Mr. Jones and are joined later by Denny's mother. The doctor tells them that Mr. Jones will recover from his injuries, but he wants to get in touch with Mr.

Jones's daughter about something else that he won't share with them.

Spence and Denny go over to the boat to find out the daughter's name from the class picture. It is listed as Flemming, not Jones. In the morning, Denny calls Andrea Flemming in Manhattan and gets an answering machine. Andrea calls later to say she'll be on the next plane.

Denny's mother meets Andrea at the airport, and Andrea explains that her father, known to them as Mr. Jones, is really Alexander Flemming. Mr. Flemming has bone cancer and needs to have an operation and undergo chemotherapy. Andrea says she's going to make her father return with her to New York for treatment.

The next day Mr. Jones tells Denny that he met Rufus Day twenty-five years ago, and that he was sure Rufus was going into the Bermuda Triangle through a time warp and into another dimension. His ship logs this spot at 75 degrees 54 minutes north latitude, 25 degrees 47 minutes west longitude. Mr. Jones wants to try to go to the same spot.

Spence tells Denny that they have to get Mr. Jones out of the hospital. Spence explains that if Mr. Jones goes back for the operation, he'll lose his leg, and there's no guarantee he'll ever get well. What Mr. Jones really wants is to go to sea on the *Misty Day*. Denny realizes she has selfishly wanted to have Mr. Jones take the place of her father.

Denny and Spence sneak Mr. Jones out of the hospital. He gets to his boat and is ready to leave. But before he goes, he gives Spence and Denny some papers. His daughter, Andrea, realizing that her father has a right to lead his life as he wishes, comes to say good-bye to him.

Mr. Jones sails off on the *Misty Day*. The papers give Spence title to the jeep. Denny is given the deed to Little Hog Island, and she and her mother decide to stay. Denny writes to her friend, who will come and visit them in a place that Denny has finally decided isn't so bad after all.

## 📖 Discussion Starters 📖

*The Last Voyage of the Misty Day*
by Jackie French Koller

**1** When the story begins, Denny has moved from an apartment in a big city to a small house by the water in an isolated area. What are some of the complaints Denny has about this move? If you were in her situation, what would you miss most if you moved from your home to a place like Phinney's Island?

**2** The Townsend family has some special Christmas traditions. What are the traditions mentioned in the story? Does your family have some special holiday traditions? What are they?

**3** Denny finds it hard to make new friends at school. She thinks that the new kids she meets dress and talk strangely. Have you ever found yourself in a situation where you felt like an "outsider"? What was it like? What did you do to become a part of the group?

**4** There have been a lot of stories told about strange adventures in time that involve the Bermuda Triangle. Why do you suppose so many of these stories are set in this same general place? Are there unusual winds or currents there? Is there something special about this spot?

**5** Denny leaps to the conclusion that because she saw a red boat, it was Spence who had beaten up Mr. Jones. Even though she falsely accuses him, Spence immediately forgives her. Is this believable? If you were Spence, how would you have reacted?

**6** Denny changes from a boyish character to a pretty girl who thinks she's in love by the end of the book. What are some of the changes that you noticed and how are they presented in the book?

**7** Denny almost drowns during an incident in the last half of the book. She recalls what Mr. Jones told her about being born knowing how to swim and that all she had to do was just get over being afraid. Why do you think the author included this incident at this point in the story?

**8** Mr. Jones says that the gulls are a lot like the people who live in Maine. They might prefer a warm June day, but they take what they get and make the best of it. He calls them "stoic." Denny calls them "stupid." How would you describe people who live in an isolated spot and endure severe weather?

**9** Andrea Flemming at first thinks that the sensible thing to do is to take her father back to New York for an operation and chemotherapy. Spence and Denny come to think that the best thing to do is to let Mr. Jones sail about on the *Misty Day* and fulfill his dream. Which do you think is best? Why?

**10** Denny ends up owning an island. Her mother has successfully found a publisher for her book. Where do you think Denny and her mother will be living and what will they be doing ten years from the end of the book? Why do you think this?

## 📖 Multidisciplinary Activities 📖

*The Last Voyage of the Misty Day*
by Jackie French Koller

**1** Andrea Flemming comes from New York City to Machias, Maine, to see her father when he is in the hospital. Use a road map to find the shortest way to travel by car from one spot to the other. Mark the route you have selected on a map. How far is it? If Andrea wanted to fly from New York City, to which city in Maine would she fly that has a big airport? From that city, how far would it be to drive in a rental car the rest of the way to Machias?

**2** When something goes wrong with the *Misty Day*'s distributor, Denny temporarily fixes it with a rubber band. What is a distributor? How does it work? Bring in a distributor to class and explain its workings, or draw a diagram of a distributor and use it to show the class what it does.

**3** Mr. Jones adds to the Thanksgiving feast by collecting mussels. Where are mussels commonly found? Are there different ways to prepare them? Bring in several recipes that call for mussels. If mussels are readily available where you live, plan a way to cook some and share them with the class.

# 📖 *Stormsearch*

by Robert Westall
New York: Farrar, Straus & Giroux, 1990. 124p.

**Type of Book:**
This book is a modern mystery, with overlays of historical fiction, told in the first person from the point of view of Tim Vaux.

**Setting:**
The story takes place near Mount House on the English seacoast.

**Major Characters:**
Tim Vaux; Tim's sister, Tracey; Tim and Tracey's Uncle Geoff and Aunt Megan; Deborah Owen, down from London to sell off an old boat collection; and Barney, who works at the Exeter boat museum.

**Other Books by the Author:**
*Demons and Shadows: The Ghostly Best Stories of Robert Westall* (New York: Farrar, Straus & Giroux, 1991), *Echoes of War* (New York: Farrar, Straus & Giroux, 1991), and *The Kingdom by the Sea* (New York: Farrar, Straus & Giroux, 1991).

## —PLOT SUMMARY—

As the book begins, a storm is brewing, but Tracey and Tim, who are visiting Mount House for their summer vacation, don't worry because the walls of Mount House are three feet thick, and there is a warm fire burning in the hearth.

Each retreats into a private world. Tracey pretends to be on a ship called the *Dawn-treader* and Tim pores over old maps. In the meantime, Uncle Geoff brings in an old clock to repair on the library table. Uncle Geoff is famous for his clock mending and his payment policy: he prefers to be paid in antiques, which Aunt Megan calls rubbish.

The morning after the storm, Uncle Geoff and Tim go to the beach and find that, like the storm of 1968, this big storm has washed away most of the sand. They find many sea creatures, some living and some dead. Uncle Geoff finds an eighteenth-century rusted iron ingot just before Tracey arrives to join them. She insists on building a sand castle.

As Tim is digging a hole in the sand, he strikes a piece of wood. It turns out to be neither a treasure chest nor a land mine, but a model ship about three feet long. At that point, the tide starts coming in. Uncle Geoff says if they rush to uncover the galleon, they'll break it. But they know that if they leave it, the tide will wash over it again.

Uncle Geoff sends Tim back to the stable to bring him a fence post, which he uses to mark the spot. They intend to come back the next day to rescue every piece of the old galleon. Uncle Geoff spends the rest of the afternoon gathering up miscellaneous equipment they will need.

The following morning, they bring all sorts of supplies to the beach including a stretcher, polythene, a petrol-driven pump, sieves, and a pile of trowels, teaspoons, and items from Aunt Megan's kitchen. Tom, Jim, and Barney, all friends of Uncle Geoff, come to help. In eight hours, they successfully complete their excavation of the ship.

The next day, Tim gets to see the ship in the coach house, where Uncle Geoff is cleaning it and allowing it to dry slowly so that it won't crack. It is made of one piece of oak. Uncle Geoff says he'll need to make new masts and sails. In the meantime, Uncle Geoff's friend Barney takes some of the bits and pieces to the Exeter boat museum to study.

For the next ten days, Uncle Geoff is on the phone or locked up in his workshop working on the ship. He finds a few faded letters of the ship's name, a *ben* and an *r*, and thinks the name might be *Ebenezer*. From the type of cloth in the sail remnant, Uncle Geoff learns the ship is a Victorian collier-brig and thinks the ship was caught in a storm and buried the same night.

In the lead ballast in the hull of the ship, Uncle Geoff finds a handmade tube containing a letter from someone named Henrietta, a letter that had gone undiscovered more than 100 years. Henrietta's letter tells about meeting someone and mentions a box hidden "under the Admiral."

Uncle Geoff thinks that the model ship was used to carry messages back and forth between two lovers, Henrietta and Humbert. He theorizes that a storm caught the ship, and the last message was never delivered.

That night, Tracey comes to Tim's room and they talk about Henrietta and Humbert. Tracey raises the question of how a Victorian girl could be playing with large model ships. She wonders if the person named Alan mentioned in the letter helps her.

A launch dinner is held before putting the restored *Ebenezer* into the water. Members of the town's boat museum attend the dinner. The next morning, family and friends launch the *Ebenezer* into the cove, but she sails clumsily and keeps washing up on shore. Uncle Geoff is angry, but Barney insists it will just take patience to get the sails right. Barney keeps at it and finally gets the ship to sail. He concludes the ship must have been headed straight for Mount Cove when it sank.

Barney asks Uncle Geoff if anyone in his family was named Humbert. Uncle Geoff now begins to dig into the family

history trying to locate such a man. Uncle Geoff Vaux learns that Humbert appeared to be one of the wild Vauxes who drank, chased women, and got into fights. He was sent out to Canada in disgrace and received a monthly remittance from his father.

In this section on family history, the reader learns more about Tim and Tracey's parents. They spend every summer going to third-world countries as part of Green Miracle, an organization that encourages governments to grow wheat and rice. Tim is bitter because whenever he leaves food on his plate, his parents remind him about starving people all over the world. It seems to Tim that his parents have little interest in him.

Tracey adores the old picture of Humbert they find and asks if she can put it in her room. She says that there's another picture of him in the house and shows it to them. Uncle Geoff agrees they must look deeper into his history.

Tim, Tracey, and their aunt and uncle go to Mountville Church to try to learn more about Henrietta, but fail. They decide to sail the *Ebenezer* to see if it will lead them to its launching place. The *Ebenezer* flies across the water, and Tim and the others have to row fast to keep up with her. But instead of leading them to a fancy house, the ship goes straight to shore in front of a set of bungalows.

There they find an old, private jetty. Uncle Geoff and Tim get out to explore, while the others row home. They finally find the remnants of Gower Park, owned by the wealthy Owen family.

By the next day, Uncle Geoff has a copy of the Ordnance Survey Map of 1872, which shows Gower Park. He also has a picture of Idris Owen, who belonged to the Secluded Brotherhood, which meant that Henrietta would have gone to church three times each Sunday but never would have been allowed to go to dances or parties.

The next day, Uncle Geoff and Tim go back to explore the area where Gower Park once was. They come upon a small house still surviving on the estate. Deborah Owen, an art student down from London, lets them in, and they learn that the house is filled with model ships. Uncle Geoff says the house should be turned into a museum, but Deborah says she'd rather chop everything up than have a museum honoring the man she calls Black Idris.

Uncle Geoff offers to bring Deborah home to stay with him while he makes arrangements to sell the ships. Uncle Geoff also says he may write a book about Black Idris. Deborah agrees to give him access to the family papers if he promises to write a true account.

Inside the model ship *Rueben* they find a note from Humbert to Henrietta. It suggests that they sail away and make a new life together. Deborah has never heard mention of a Henrietta in the family, so Uncle Geoff begins to search through the papers.

Aunt Megan also begins to investigate and learns that the Secluded Brethren, members of the Brotherhood, have a chapel in the little village of Summergrove, which they visit. In the "wrong" side of the graveyard they find the grave of Henrietta Mary Owen, who died at eighteen, only two days after writing the letter that they discovered in the *Ebenezer*.

They return to the house in Gower Park and continue to read through the family papers. They find a music case with torn-up photographs in it. Tracey hopes to find the buried treasure beneath the "Admiral" that Henrietta mentioned in her note. In the old account papers, they find an entry to pay the men who found Henrietta's body in the sea.

The only "Admiral" they can locate is a fairly modern pub called The Admiral at Turton. Tracey insists that they go there. A customer tells them there was an older inn up a side road. They go up and find the ruins, then return to the house.

There they find another music case of torn photographs. One shows Henrietta with the little ship *Ebenezer*. Behind her is a man they suspect is the helpful Alan that she and Humbert mention in their letters. There is also an old newspaper account of the wreck of the *Brutus*. The account describes how Humbert went out

to try to save passengers and how Henrietta fell to her death from the cliffs while watching the rescue attempt in the gale.

E C Proby arrives from Sotheby's and says that the Idris Owen collection might be worth more than 200,000 pounds. Uncle Goeff, E C Proby, and the others go to the pub in the rain, and while there begin talking about the buried treasure beneath the Admiral. E C Proby suggests that old oak trees are sometimes called "Admirals."

Uncle Geoff takes Deborah and E C Proby off to see his collections. Aunt Megan takes Tracey shopping. Tim is left alone in the house, and he goes up to the tower, where he dreams of the country as it was 100 years ago. Tim sees the little boat and galloping horses headed for the inn. He sees Henrietta on the cliff, looking toward the land, waiting for someone. Then he is awakened when the others come back.

The next day, Deborah, Uncle Geoff, and Tim go to the oak stump on the grounds of the old inn. As they are searching, the landowner drives up. They decide not to dig until two o'clock in the morning on a Sunday so that no one will see them. They dig on Sunday and find the chest, but it crumbles to dust when they touch it. All they find is a locket and some pearls.

It is the last day of summer vacation for Tim and Tracey, so Aunt Megan packs a picnic lunch and Uncle Geoff takes a day off from his papers to sail the model ship, the *Nathaniel*, which he's bought from Deborah. They all go out in a little boat and then set the *Nathaniel* into the water.

Winds come up, and the *Nathaniel* streaks away from them. They follow and eventually come upon a little cove just beyond Mount Castle, where they picnic. While the adults are resting and talking in the sun, Tracey sees something up on the cliffs and gets Tim to check into it for her. It is a rusty, cast-iron memorial to Henrietta, put there by the faithful Alan, saying that she felt abandoned and jumped from the cliff. Everyone is satisfied now that they have solved the old mystery.

# 📖 Discussion Starters 📖

*Stormsearch*
by Robert Westall

**1** This story takes place during a summer vacation which Tim and Tracey spend with their aunt and uncle. At the end of the story, Tim wishes he could stay with his aunt and uncle but admits that he might get as tired of them as he was of his parents when he left home. From what you have learned about the characters, do you think that Tim would have been happiest living with his parents or his aunt and uncle? Why? With whom would you rather live?

**2** In the beginning of the story, it seems that Tim's little sister, Tracey, is just an annoyance or tag-along character. But as the story develops, she has a major role to play. Refer to the text and discuss the major contributions that Tracey makes as the plot develops.

**3** This story is set in England. The language has a slightly different flavor from that in stories written by Americans. What are some of the words or phrases that you noticed in the book that made it stand out as an English story?

**4** The relationship between Uncle Geoff and Aunt Megan is a complex one. At times, each one supports or irritates the other. From what you read, which of the two do you think is the most tolerant and makes the most allowances for the other? What leads you to think this?

**5** Although Black Idris has died long before this story begins, he is in some ways a main character in the story. How many different ways can you find in which the author revealed information about Black Idris? From these bits and pieces, what can you say about this character?

**6** E C Proby is an unusual character who enters late in the book. We do not know her first name and no punctuation is used after her initials. Why was this character introduced in this way? Would it have made a difference in the book if an Edward Charles Proby arrived to buy the antique ship collection? What would the differences be?

**7** When recovering the contents of Henrietta's box, Deborah says that she thinks it's like "opening a grave." What are the factors involved that call up that emotion?

**8** With the first message found in the *Ebenezer*, there is reference to a box buried under the Admiral. Were you expecting that Tim would ever find this box? What did you think would be inside it? Were you satisfied or disappointed when the box was finally opened?

**9** Uncle Geoff characterizes himself as a "bad Vaux." Is that an appropriate or inappropriate name for him? What personal characteristics, both good and bad, does Uncle Geoff possess? Cite references from the story to justify your assessment. Overall, would you consider him to be a good or a bad Vaux?

**10** On the last page of the book, Tim asks an interesting question: "Which was more important, the starving millions of Asia, or Henrietta Owen and her brave fight for freedom?" How would *you* answer that question?

# □ **Multidisciplinary Activities** □

*Stormsearch*
by Robert Westall

**1** Uncle Geoff learns that the model ship he and Tim found, the *Ebenezer*, is a "collier-brig." What sort of ship was this? When was it used? For what purpose was it used? Make a line drawing of a collier-brig. Share your picture with your classmates and explain to them the history of this type of vessel.

**2** E C Proby is a representative from Sotheby's who has come to give an estimate of the value at auction of the model ships in the Gower Park house. Sotheby's is especially well known. What is it? Where is it? How does it function? Share what you learn with your classmates.

**3** Sometimes, out of curiosity or need, it is important to learn more about a piece of property that may have been sold and may have changed hands many times. Choose a piece of historical property in your community. Delve into its history. Where will you go to find records about who first owned it and what was built on it? Where will you find records about the number of times it was sold and the various owners up to the present? Share what you learn and your methods of research with your class.

# The True Confessions of Charlotte Doyle

by Avi Wortis
New York: Orchard Books, 1990. 215p.

**Type of Book:**
This is an historical work of fiction set in the year 1832, told in the first person by a thirteen-year-old girl.

**Setting:**
Most of the story takes place aboard a ship called the *Seahawk* during a crossing of the Atlantic Ocean.

**Major Characters:**
Charlotte Doyle; Zachariah, an old, black sailor; Mr. Jaggery, captain of the *Seahawk*; and Mr. Keetch, a mate on the ship.

**Other Books by the Author:**
*Bright Shadow* (New York: Bradbury Press, 1985), *City of Light, City of Dark: A Comic Book Novel* (New York: Orchard Books, 1993), and *Who Was That Masked Man, Anyway?* (New York: Orchard Books, 1992).

## —PLOT SUMMARY—

This book begins with a warning from Charlotte Doyle saying she is going to tell this tale exactly as she lived it. Charlotte explains that she was born in America but spent the years between her sixth and thirteenth birthdays in England, where her father was engaged in the manufacture of cotton goods.

In the spring of 1832, Charlotte's father was promoted and summoned home. It was decided that Charlotte would finish her term at school and then follow her mother, father, younger brother, and sister home to Providence, Rhode Island, during the summer. The plan was for her to sail on a ship owned by her father's firm. Two families had also booked passage on the ship and would serve as her guardians. Charlotte's father gives her a blank journal and encourages her to record the events of the crossing.

On the day she is to set sail, Charlotte meets Mr. Grummage, who takes her down to the ship and explains that although he had thought the departure would be delayed, Captain Jaggery has informed him they'll sail the next morning. Two porters carrying Charlotte's luggage flee when they learn they are headed for the *Seahawk*, a ship captained by Mr. Jaggery.

Charlotte waits while Mr. Grummage goes on board the ship. He reappears and tells Charlotte he has learned that the other two families are not coming, but he insists that she go aboard, even though she protests that it would not be right for a girl to be sailing with an all-male crew. Mr. Grummage says that she must sail, as he is leaving for Scotland. So Charlotte Doyle boards the brig *Seahawk* on June 16, 1832.

Both the captain and first mate are ashore when Charlotte boards, and the second mate, Mr. Keetch, is in charge. Mr. Keetch suggests that Charlotte take another ship, but Mr. Grummage won't hear of a change in plans.

Mr. Keetch leads Charlotte to her cabin. There is no window, and the room is so small that there is no room for her trunk. When Barlow, a seaman, brings the trunk, he too advises Charlotte to return to shore. Zachariah, an old, black sailor, appears and offers to take her to have tea in the galley. He offers to be her friend. He gives her tea and also a knife.

The crew is a motley collection of men. The first mate, Mr. Hollybrass, explains that they are shorthanded because no one else will sign articles to serve as crew on the ship. Charlotte meets Captain Andrew Jaggery, believes he is a gentleman, and states that she wishes to return to land and shouldn't be aboard, but he dismisses her. Quite seasick, Charlotte takes to her bed.

After four days of illness, Charlotte goes to the kitchen to see Zachariah and to return his knife to him. He gives her tea and hardtack. Zachariah tells her that on a previous voyage, a Mr. Cranick didn't tie a knot to please the captain, so the captain beat him. No one else will sign on except for the original crew, which is seeking revenge against the captain.

Charlotte visits the captain in his handsome cabin. She offers him the knife but says it was given to her by Mr. Grummage. The captain tells her to keep it and shows her a round robin. He advises her to tell him if she ever sees one.

The captain shows her a picture of his five-year-old daughter and tries to be charming and friendly to Charlotte. He makes a display of walking with her on deck and has his mate call Barlow to take her to her trunk.

While checking in her trunk, Charlotte sees two faces before her candle is snuffed out. In the semidarkness she realizes that one face is a carving of some kind, but the other face has disappeared. Charlotte takes some of her clothes and a book from her trunk back to her cabin.

After a week, Charlotte settles into her routine. On Sundays, she reads a short message from the Bible during services. For half an hour a day, Charlotte takes tea with the captain. She gradually gets to know the crew, asks questions, runs errands, and listens to their stories.

She also notices that the captain keeps the men constantly busy and often punishes them for small infractions.

Consequently, the crew begin to grumble. When Mr. Ewing, a seaman, breaks his needle while mending, Charlotte offers to get him another. When she does so, she overhears the crew members planning something. She also sees a pistol in Mr. Ewing's trunk. A round robin that was on the trunk falls to the floor.

Charlotte is not certain what she should do. In reflecting on what she's seen in the forecastle, she comes to believe that there is a stowaway on board. Charlotte hurries off to tell the captain but meets Morgan, another member of the crew, who looks at her and draws his finger across his throat in what she takes to be a warning.

Charlotte, nonetheless, goes to the captain and tells him everything. The captain, armed and accompanied by Mr. Hollybrass, summons the crew. Mr. Keetch appears, and then the rest of the crew, armed with guns and knives, along with the stowaway, Mr. Cranick. When Mr. Cranick demands justice, the captain shoots him in the chest.

Zachariah goes to help in spite of the captain's action, but Mr. Cranick is dead. The captain has him thrown overboard. Then he asks Charlotte to choose one other crew member to be punished. Charlotte refuses, so the captain has Zachariah strung up by his wrists and orders fifty lashes. Charlotte throws herself against Mr. Hollybrass and takes the whip. In so doing, she accidentally hits the captain with it. The captain then beats Zachariah. After he leaves, the crew cuts him down.

Charlotte goes to the captain to beg forgiveness but is met with hatred and told never to come there again. Then she comes upon Zachariah's funeral. The captain calls everyone on deck, demotes Mr. Keetch, promotes Mr. Johnson, a seaman who did not sign the round robin, and assigns Mr. Fisk, another seaman, to take over the kitchen chores.

Charlotte puts on a sailor suit that Zachariah had made for her earlier and reports to the kitchen to be part of the crew. Mr. Fisk takes her to the others.

They decide that if she is able to climb to the royal yard and come down unharmed, they'll accept her on the crew.

She agrees to climb the 130-foot mast. It takes a long time, and once she falls and is caught by the ropes, but Charlotte makes the climb up and down. Then the captain appears. She tells him of her intentions, and he says that from now on she will simply be considered to be a crew member named Mr. Doyle.

The crew members teach her what they can and give her a bunk in the forecastle that affords some privacy. The captain continues to try to find fault with her. One day he directs her to fix the bowsprit. Charlotte manages to accomplish this but almost falls into the ocean. Instead of being pleased, the captain strikes her for causing them to temporarily change course, and she denounces him.

The next day the crew sees a strange bird. Barlow calls it a blood bird from the Caribbean and says it has been blown there by a hurricane. When the hurricane strikes, the captain sends Charlotte up to cut the foreyard sail away. She almost falls but is saved by a figure that she thinks is Zachariah, who is thought to be dead. During the eye of the storm, they discover Mr. Hollybrass dead, with a knife in his back and Charlotte's handkerchief in his hand.

Charlotte sleeps for fourteen hours because no one calls her to come on watch. She learns that the captain has accused her of murder and that she'll stand trial on ship. She is put in the brig. Zachariah comes to talk to her. He tells her that he did not die and that he has hidden in the hold since the mock funeral. The other men know he is alive and have given him food and water. When they land, he will sneak off the ship and report on the captain. Charlotte does not know if it is Zachariah or someone else who has killed the first mate.

The captain comes down and brings Charlotte on deck for a trial. He convicts her while the men say nothing to defend her. He sentences her to be hanged in twenty-four hours. Charlotte goes back to the brig, where she and Zachariah finally decide that the captain has murdered Mr. Hollybrass. They also think he has seen Zachariah, that he plans to kill his first mate, hang Charlotte, and then deal with Zachariah.

Zachariah convinces Charlotte that she must get the guns because she knows where the key to them is hidden in the captain's cabin. Once the captain does not have a gun, the crew will rally again. Zachariah tells Mr. Keetch what has really happened, and they work out a plan, but Mr. Keetch snitches to the captain.

When Charlotte goes to the captain's cabin, he is waiting for her. He offers to hang her, to give her her clothes if she promises to keep quiet when they dock, or to let her take his gun so that he will be murdered and her family's name ruined.

Charlotte runs out on the deck. The crew will not help her. The captain shoots at her but misses. In chasing her out onto the bowsprit, he falls into the ocean. Charlotte is made captain in name, though in reality, Zachariah fills the role. They agree to say that the captain and mate were lost in the storm.

When they land, Charlotte is met by her family. They are surprised at her appearance, but they take Charlotte home and try to force her quickly back into a normal lifestyle, despite the tales Charlotte tells of her journey. Her father burns her journal, and she is confined to her room. She bribes a servant to bring her newspapers. When she learns that the *Seahawk* is about to sail, Charlotte slips off in the middle of the night to rejoin Zachariah and the crew.

## 📖 Discussion Starters 📖

*The True Confessions of Charlotte Doyle*
by Avi Wortis

**1** How does the title of this book, the footnotes that define special sea terms, and the material in the appendix all work together to influence how the reader reacts to this story?

**2** Find the description of the figurehead on the *Seahawk* and reread it. What is the function of this description? How does it work to give the reader clues about what is to come?

**3** Zachariah describes himself as cook, surgeon, carpenter, and preacher to man, ship, and Charlotte. Was it common on board a ship for one person to try to be all these things? What are some of the actions of Zachariah throughout the story that prove he is more than a cook?

**4** The knife, or dirk, plays a major role in this story. Trace the dirk throughout the story, from when it was first introduced to its final use as a murder weapon. If you had been given the dirk by Zachariah, what would you have done with it?

**5** In discussing the captain's punishment of Mr. Cranick, Zachariah asks if Charlotte believes in justice. She says she is an American. When Zachariah says, "Ah! Justice for all?" Charlotte answers, "For those who deserve it." What do you think Charlotte meant by this? What do you think "justice" means?

**6** Find several instances throughout the book where Charlotte indicates that she thinks she is "better" than the crew and distances herself and avoids mingling with them. How does this aspect of Charlotte's character affect what happens in the last half of the book?

**7** Review the scene where Mr. Cranick is killed and thrown overboard. What does that scene reveal about the following characters: the captain, Zachariah, Charlotte, and Mr. Hollybrass?

**8** Why do you think the crew chooses to have Charlotte prove herself by climbing as high as the royal yard before permitting her to be a crew member? What function does this climb play in the story?

**9** After Charlotte has been accused of murder, she is given the choice of withdrawing from the crew and "hiding behind her father's name," preventing the captain from judging her in his court. She chooses to trust the crew, but no one speaks for her. If you were placed in Charlotte's situation, what would you have done and why?

**10** The captain is lost at sea while climbing out on the bowsprit and trying to murder Charlotte. Yet, when he falls, she reaches out and catches his hand, though finally she cannot save him. Why do you think the author included this scene?

---

## 📖 **Multidisciplinary Activities** 📖

### *The True Confessions of Charlotte Doyle*
### by Avi Wortis

**1** Charlotte sets sail on June 16, 1832, for Providence, Rhode Island. Do some historical research. What was Providence like in 1832? What were its major industries? How many people lived in Providence then compared with its population today? What major events, political and otherwise, happened in Rhode Island in 1832? Share with your class what you learned and how you did your historical research.

**2** Space on the *Seahawk* is at a premium. Charlotte's room is so small that she cannot even keep her trunk in it. Suppose you are designing the best use of space for the sleeping deck; you have an area to work with that is 130 feet long and 30 feet wide, with a 3-foot aisle down the middle and a ladder at each end leading up to the deck. How can you design the sleeping deck so that it will accommodate the largest number of crew members while still providing each crew member with a room of at least 32 square feet? Try different arrangements. Share your best floor plan with the class.

**3** British schoolchildren often had to solve example arithmetic problems that might later be useful to them in such an occupation as shipping clerk. The cargo of a ship is often given in the unit "tons." A problem such as the following might appear in an early British arithmetic book:

Add 5 1/2 long hundredweight to 4.125 long quarter-tons and reduce the result to a decimal in the unit "long tons."

Can you solve this problem? (**Hint**—1 long hundredweight equals 112 pounds and 1 long ton equals 20 long hundredweight.)

---

# 📖 *Bridge* 📖

## Ships, Diving, and Treasure

---

### ◆ Literature Books ◆

📖*Beyond the Reef*
Chris moves to Florida and learns
to dive for treasure

📖*Dragon's Plunder*
Pirates and more pirates, for fantasy lovers

📖*The Last Voyage of the Misty Day*
Denny's adventures on an island
off the coast of Maine

📖*Stormsearch*
A mystery with a touch of history
on the coast of England

📖*The True Confessions of Charlotte Doyle*
The adventures of 13-year-old Charlotte
as she crosses the Atlantic in 1832

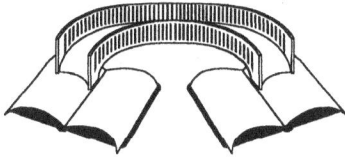

---

### ◆ Bridge ◆

📖*Night Dive*
Adventures while scuba
diving at night on a coral
reef

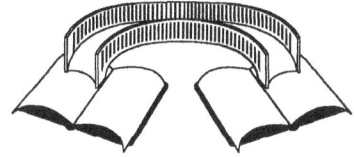

---

### ◆ Nonfiction Connections ◆

📖*Diving for Treasure*
For serious divers only

📖*Diving to the Past: Recovering Ancient Wrecks*
Salvaging ancient wrecks with
conservational concern

📖*Footsteps in the Ocean: Careers in Diving*
Diving for sport and business

📖*The Lost Wreck of the Isis*
The JASON project and its deep-sea discoveries

📖*Mysteries of the Deep*
A challenging book of sunken
treasures, mysterious voyages,
strange creatures, and unexplained disappearances

📖*Shipwrecks: Terror and Treasure*
Three famous shipwrecks, and the
dives to photograph and recover
their treasures

📖*Sunken Ships & Treasure*
Famous shipwrecks and treasure
hunts

#### OTHER TOPICS TO EXPLORE

| | | |
|---|---|---|
| —Lighthouses | —Types of sailing vessels | —Sonar |
| —Doctors who dive | —Ship models | —The Bermuda Triangle |
| —Salvage | —Wrecks on shipping lanes | —Maritime museums |
| —Propulsion | —Recovering ancient wrecks | —Ship graveyards |
| —Privateers | —Underwater photography | —Spanish galleons |

# 📖 *Night Dive*

by Ann McGovern
New York: Macmillan, 1984. 56p.

This is a fairly short, easy-to-read book that contains approximately half text and half color photographs. The book focuses on nighttime on a coral reef, when many creatures not seen during the day emerge to hunt for food.

Although this is essentially a nonfiction book, the various sections of the book are unified by a story line describing a series of true-life night-diving adventures, which makes this a good book to bridge from fiction to nonfiction. Told in the first person, a twelve-year-old girl shares her thoughts about making a night scuba dive with a small group of people.

The young scuba diver is frightened at first but then becomes so engrossed in the many creatures that she sees, including a stingray, moray eels, a barracuda, basket stars, and parrot fish, that she forgets her fear. Gradually, she comes to feel at home in the water and in her gear and to love night diving.

At one point during a dive, the young diver's light fails, and she briefly finds herself alone in the dark waters. She learns that a twilight dive is particularly rich in sea creatures because it reveals creatures active in the daytime as well as those that start coming out at night. A few of the potential dangers of diving are also pointed out as the young diver survives bumping into a giant sea bass inside an old shipwreck, meeting an octopus, and surfacing without being stung by sea wasps.

## Possible Topics for Further Student Investigation

1 After the age of twelve, it is possible to earn a scuba certification card. Find out more about becoming a certified scuba diver. What do you need to learn? What is the place nearest to where you live that offers scuba diving certification? Do some research to locate a certified scuba diver in your area. Invite a certified scuba diver to visit your class. Ask the diver to bring in diving gear and to discuss his or her scuba diving experiences.

2 One creature that lives in the sea (and it certainly looks more like exploding fireworks or a pincushion than a fish) is the spiny sea urchin. There are many different kinds. If you are interested in sea urchins, do some library research to find out more about them. In what parts of the world are they found? How do they move? What do they eat? How do they reproduce? Do they have any economic value? Where do they fit into the food chain? What other kinds of sea creatures are closely related to the sea urchins?

3 The diver discovers that it is not silent around the sunken wreck. In fact, it is noisy. How does sound travel in the water? Why do sounds that travel in the water differ from those that travel through the air? Some of the most interesting recorded sea sounds are those made by whales. Many of these whale songs have been recorded. Bring in a recording of whale music and share it with your classmates.

# 📖 *Nonfiction Connections* 📖

## Ships, Diving, and Treasure

---

### ◆ Literature Books ◆

📖 *Beyond the Reef*
Chris moves to Florida and learns to dive for treasure

📖 *Dragon's Plunder*
Pirates and more pirates, for fantasy lovers

📖 *The Last Voyage of the Misty Day*
Denny's adventures on an island off the coast of Maine

📖 *Stormsearch*
A mystery with a touch of history on the coast of England

📖 *The True Confessions of Charlotte Doyle*
The adventures of 13-year-old Charlotte as she crosses the Atlantic in 1832

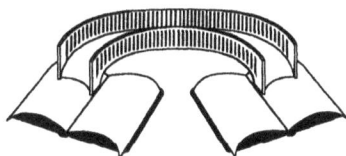

---

### ◆ Bridge ◆

📖 *Night Dive*
Adventures while scuba diving at night on a coral reef

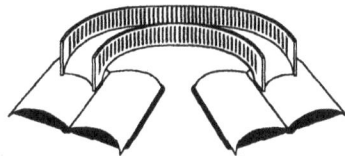

---

### ◆ Nonfiction Connections ◆

📖 *Diving for Treasure*
For serious divers only

📖 *Diving to the Past: Recovering Ancient Wrecks*
Salvaging ancient wrecks with conservational concern

📖 *Footsteps in the Ocean: Careers in Diving*
Diving for sport and business

📖 *The Lost Wreck of the Isis*
The JASON project and its deep-sea discoveries

📖 *Mysteries of the Deep*
A challenging book of sunken treasures, mysterious voyages, strange creatures, and unexplained disappearances

📖 *Shipwrecks: Terror and Treasure*
Three famous shipwrecks, and the dives to photograph and recover their treasures

📖 *Sunken Ships & Treasure*
Famous shipwrecks and treasure hunts

#### OTHER TOPICS TO EXPLORE

—Lighthouses
—Doctors who dive
—Salvage
—Propulsion
—Privateers

—Types of sailing vessels
—Ship models
—Wrecks on shipping lanes
—Recovering ancient wrecks
—Underwater photography

—Sonar
—The Bermuda Triangle
—Maritime museums
—Ship graveyards
—Spanish galleons

# 📖 *Diving for Treasure*

by Wyatt Blassingame
Philadelphia: Macrae-Smith, 1971. 147p.

---

This is a classic children's book on diving for treasure. It is mostly text, with just a few black-and-white photographs. Although there are few illustrations, the book is easy to read because most of the chapters are presented in a story format.

Chapter one is a brief history of diving from an early account of salvage diving for the Persian King Xerxes to the current oceanographic work of Jacques-Yves Cousteau.

Chapter two discusses Sir William Phips and the treasure he recovered from a sunken Spanish ship, the *Almiranta*. Chapter three deals with the discovery by some sponge divers in 1900 of the *Antikythera* wreck in the eastern Mediter-

ranean. The wreck contained bronze statues, including one identified as the *Athlete of Antikythera*, sculpted by Lysippos in the fourth century B.C.

Chapter four discusses the work of Peter Throckmorton in 1959 off the coast of Turkey at Cape Gelidonya. His group of divers took many photographs of human-made implements and brought up a few pieces of bronze which were identified as belonging to the late Bronze Age, sometime between 1300 B.C. and 1200 B.C.

Later chapters deal with the search for treasure off the coasts of Florida and California and of sunken treasure that was the result of the world wars.

## Possible Topics for Further Student Investigation

1 Many, many stories have been written about diving and the recovery of sunken treasure. To make such a story a success, even one that is fictional, the writer often must study history. There must be an accurate discussion of the boats and type of diving equipment used and an explanation of the historical events surrounding the sinking of the ship. Write your own short story about diving for sunken treasure. Set it in whatever time period you wish, but be sure that the information is based on fact.

2 One of the best-known names connected with the sea is that of Jacques-Yves Cousteau. With Emil Gagnan, Cousteau perfected the first effective scuba (self-contained underwater breathing apparatus)—the Aqua Lung—which allowed divers to swim and breathe beneath the surface of the water. Research the development of scuba equipment. How has it changed over the years? What is state-of-the-art scuba equipment like today? Share your library research in a report to your class.

3 In reading about treasure beneath the sea, you often hear about gold bricks. For example, 3,211 gold bricks sank on the *Laurentic* when it struck a German mine off the coast of Ireland and sank. Do some research to share with your class. What are the dimensions of one of these gold bricks? Are they a standard size? How much is each brick worth? How much does such a gold brick weigh? Is the currency of the United States still backed with gold? What form is that gold in, and where is it stored? Prepare some math problems about gold bricks for your classmates to solve.

---

# 📖 *Diving to the Past: Recovering Ancient Wrecks*

by W. John Hackwell
New York: Charles Scribner's Sons, 1988. 54p.

---

This is a short book with easy-to-read text that is illustrated with pastel sketches. Hackwell explains how ancient ships are salvaged and what they tell us about the past.

The book is divided into seven chapters. The first chapter, "Treasure Under the Sea," begins by describing how as early as 4500 B.C., divers were bringing up shells to be used for purple dyes for royal garments. It continues up to and through modern expeditions.

In "Dangers of the Deep," the author discusses such problems as huge swells and tidal surges. The chapter "Searching for Lost Wrecks" details how computers are used to record information about dives, how magnetometers are used to detect masses of ferrous metals, and what techniques are involved in recovery and display.

Other chapters are "The Dive Team" and "Underwater Excavation Begins." Included in these are descriptions of the work of photographers, surveyors, divers, and computer operators.

The final two chapters are "Preserving Ancient Wrecks" and "Saving the Future." Field conservation, treatment of objects after they have been moved from a stable underwater environment, and the dangers of corrosion, explosives, and so on are examined. Finally, there is an emphasis on the importance of maritime museums and marine archaeology as a means of preserving for the future our understanding of the past.

## Possible Topics for Further Student Investigation

1 This book suggests that computers can play a major role in various aspects of recovering ancient wrecks. It shows how a drawing of a ship can be superimposed on a computer grid so that artifacts recovered from underwater can be listed and numbered according to their underwater positions. Create a computer program that could be used for this function. Make a drawing of an imaginary ship and the area immediately around it. Superimpose it on a grid structure and locate at least six artifacts. Share your program with your class.

2 Along with this book's explanation of the various skills that a diving team might have, there is a sketch showing a diver using a sextant. What is the purpose of a sextant? How does it work? Either bring a sextant into the classroom and explain its use to your classmates or make a detailed diagram showing its parts and how it is used.

3 People who dive are in a physically demanding occupation. This book points out that well-planned meals and a well-stocked galley are critical to the well-being of the divers and the success of the diving expedition. Suppose you were in charge of planning the meals for a crew of six people on a dive boat that would be at sea for a week. Remember that you will have limited refrigerated space. You need to include variety and be concerned with good nutrition. What would you include? How many calories would be included in each day's meals? Make a week-long menu listing each day's foods. You may use catchy titles for entrees if you wish!

From *Bridges to the World of Water*. © 1995. Teacher Ideas Press. (800) 237-6124.

# 📖 *Footsteps in the Ocean: Careers in Diving*

by Denise V. Lang
New York: E. P. Dutton, 1987. 144p.

This book is mostly print with just a few black-and-white photographs. The author suggests that careers in diving have greatly expanded in recent years and now involve such diverse activities as diving to retrieve criminal evidence, diving in connection with oil rigs, diving as a marine biologist, or diving as a cinematographer.

Part one of the book is devoted to sport diving. It examines such careers as dive instructor, dive master, diving-resort manager, dive journalist, underwater photographer, underwater cinematographer, and diving and its connection to the retail industry.

Part two explores commercial diving, including the careers of commercial air diver, bell saturation diver, ROV (Remotely Operated Vehicle) technician, and salvage diver. Although these are thought by some to be less glamorous diving careers than those explored in part one, there may actually be more opportunities in commercial diving.

Science and research comprise part three, where the careers of marine biologist, marine ecologist, diver medic, physician diver, and underwater archaeologist are discussed.

The final section of the book considers diving in connection with police search and recovery as well as in the military. A list of schools, diving associations, and publications is included.

## Possible Topics for Further Student Investigation

1. Almost every part of the country has dive shops or a travel agency that specializes in dive trips. Contact one of these and locate a resource person who is willing to come and visit your school. The diver could talk about the equipment that is used and the training and certification that is necessary. The resource person might even bring in some photographs from diving trips to share with your class.

2. Publications in every field have catchy names to try to attract readers and to stand out from others in the field. For example, *The Dry Dock* is the name of a publication of Human Underwater Biology, Inc. *Undercurrent* is the name of another print guide for serious divers. Suppose you were asked to begin a magazine or newsletter that dealt with diving. On what area of diving would you focus? Select a catchy title for your publication and design an appropriate logo.

3. On January 28, 1986, the space shuttle *Challenger*, carrying the first civilian astronaut, Christa McAuliffe, a high school teacher from New Hampshire, exploded seventy-two seconds into its flight. The largest pieces of the *Challenger* lay underwater, scattered across forty miles at depths of 100 to 2,000 feet. NASA put out a call, and ROVs were put into service to search for debris. Ask your media specialist to help you research magazine articles and share what you learn about ROVs with your classmates.

# 📖 *The Lost Wreck of the Isis*
## by Robert D. Ballard
Toronto: Madison Press Books, 1990. 64p.

This is a large-format book with both color drawings and photographs. It chronicles a first-person factual account of the JASON Project and also gives a fictionalized, but fact-based story of sailing in A.D. 355.

Robert Ballard and his crew photographed the diving efforts surrounding the passenger ship *Titanic*. A year later, they returned to the Mediterranean with archaeological experts for further underwater exploration as part of the JASON Project.

The first phase of this project involved the discovery in 1988 of a Roman ship, *Isis*, that had sunk sixteen centuries ago. To find the ship, the crew depended on Argo, a deep-towed vehicle with video cameras that had found the wreck of the *Titanic*. The searchers followed trade routes near the Strait of Messina and the Strait of Sicily. When they finally located a shipwreck, they did not investigate further at the time, but simply marked the spot for their return in phase two of the project.

The second phase, carried out the following spring, used JASON, a high-tech, underwater, remote-controlled robot. Live images of the deep-sea discoveries of JASON were beamed live to students around the world at various sites, including science museums. In addition to the shipwreck, the crew also studied underwater geology.

## Possible Topics for Further Student Investigation

1. We do not have an account of the day-to-day activities that must have taken place on the ship *Isis*. The author of this book relied upon general historical information about the people, clothing, food, and other elements of the cultures of that time to create a fictionalized account of the journey. Writing such fiction takes an enormous amount of research. Choose some topic from early history that is of interest to you. Suppose you were going to write a story set in that time, fictional yet historically accurate. Do some of the initial research. Cite six sources of information that you would use.

2. Safe scuba divers dive no more than 130 feet, yet JASON can dive 20,000 feet. Clearly, advancements like JASON make underwater discoveries more likely than ever before. Find out what you can about JASON. Where was it developed? How big is it? How does it work? Share what you learn in an oral report to your class.

3. The Mediterranean Basin is a geologically complex area with a great deal of volcanic activity. It also features plates colliding and rubbing against each other. Prepare a map showing the locations of the major volcanoes in this area. Make charts to show how plate movement can lead to earthquakes like those that have frequently been experienced in California along the San Andreas Fault. Use your charts to explain to your class more about the causes of volcanic activity and earthquakes.

# 📖 *Mysteries of the Deep*

edited by Joseph J. Thorndike, Jr.
New York: American Heritage, 1980. 352p.

---

This is a rather long, adult book that will challenge young readers with sections devoted to such topics as sunken treasure, mysterious voyages, unexplained disappearances, and strange creatures in the seas. Most of the illustrations are black-and-white photographs. For a student who is really interested in this topic, however, it will prove to be a fascinating book.

The beginning of the book is devoted to sunken treasures, including lost galleons of the Spanish Main, the lost flota of 1715, the adventures of Sir William Phips, wrecks of the Spanish Armada, and the pirates of Jamaica.

The second section deals with archaeology of the Mediterranean and includes a special section of photographs of classical Greek sculptures that were preserved in and rescued from the sea and an anthology of accounts by explorers of the deep. (It is rare to find accounts from so many famous explorers included in one book.)

The next section of the book deals with mysterious voyages, disappearances, and creatures. Included here are two picture portfolios, including a marine bestiary of sea monsters. The book concludes with the section "Exploring the Ocean Floor," which includes a discussion of rivers in the ocean, great waves, and volcanoes of the Mid-Atlantic Ridge.

## Possible Topics for Further Student Investigation

**1** In the "Anthology of Accounts by Explorers of the Deep" is one by Jacques-Yves Cousteau. He tells of his worst experience, which occurred not during a dive in the sea but during a dive in an inland water cave, the Fountain of Vauchuse, near Avignon. Read the account and then report back to your class orally about this terrifying true-life adventure.

**2** A bronze head of Medusa, thought to have sunk with one of Caligula's barges, is one of the items pictured in *Mysteries of the Deep* (page 108). Who was Medusa? Research Medusa and find other depictions of her. From what you read and the art you find, design your own original image of Medusa in whatever medium you prefer. When it is complete, share your original work of art with your class. Explain why you made her look the way you did and why you chose to present Medusa in this particular art medium.

**3** After reading the section about mysterious voyages and mysterious appearances involving shipwrecks, write your own short play. Base it on some recorded account of a true mystery at sea. It does not need to be one that is included in this book. As you write your play, concentrate on realistic dialogue. Have your characters speak in ways that are appropriate for both the time and situation. With classmates reading your play, make an audio recording to share with the class. Be sure to include appropriate background music.

---

# 📖 *Shipwrecks: Terror and Treasure*

by Kathryn Long Humphrey
New York: Franklin Watts, 1991. 64p.

This is a short, easy-to-read book illustrated with color photographs. The book discusses three famous shipwrecks and the dives made to photograph and recover the treasure.

The book begins with a discussion of King Henry's warship, the *Mary Rose*, built in 1510. In 1545, loaded with heavy cannons to fight the French, the ship sank near Portsmouth, England. Alexander McKee borrowed some special equipment to help find the *Mary Rose*, a piece of which was uncovered in 1970. It was finally brought up in 1982 and is now available for public viewing.

The middle section of the book gives information about the Concepcion, a Spanish galleon that sailed from Cuba in 1641, was swept off course by a hurricane, crashed into a reef, and sank. Sir William Phips located this boat in the 1970s and removed tons of gold and silver. In 1978, Burt Webber and his crew went back to the site and brought up more treasure.

The final famous shipwreck discussed in this book is the sinking of the *Titanic* in 1912 with 2,200 people on board. Only 868 survived because there were not enough lifeboats and many ships either did not hear the call or were not close enough to respond in time. The *Carparthia* rescued 675 passengers. Robert Ballard and his crews located the *Titanic* and, using underwater robots, photographed it in 1986.

## Possible Topics for Further Student Investigation

**1** Because more than half of its passengers died, and because women and children in lifeboats watched the ship sink with husbands, brothers, and fathers on board, the sinking of the *Titanic* gave rise to the writing of many stories, poems, and ballads. One such ballad (title unknown and author anonymous) concludes with these lines:

> Poor widows and mothers dear,
> For their loved ones sadly weep,
> For those on the liner, *Titanic*,
> Now sleep in the ocean deep.

Compose a simple ballad about the sinking of this great ship. Play it on an instrument of your choice and sing it for your classmates.

**2** The curators in the *Mary Rose* museum in England faced many special problems in exhibiting the *Mary Rose* because the old ship, once preserved beneath the sand at the bottom of the channel, was exposed to various elements that would cause it to deteriorate when it was brought out of the water for millions of visitors to see. What special problems were faced and how were these problems solved so that the sailing vessel was preserved? Investigate these issues and share what you learn with your classmates.

**3** In recovering treasure from sunken ships, astrolabes are sometimes found. An astrolabe is an instrument used by ship pilots of the seventeenth century to calculate the position of the stars so that they could navigate. Find out more about astrolabes. What did they look like? How did they work? What other navigation instruments were used by early sailors? Explain the use of astrolabes to your classmates.

# 📖 *Sunken Ships & Treasure*

by John Christopher Fine
New York: Atheneum, 1986. 119p.

This book, illustrated with color photographs, is easy to read and was an International Oceanographic Foundation selection.

Various sunken ships and treasures are featured in this book. It begins with a discussion of three sites where treasure hunters have been at work. The first is the Anegada Passage, a fifteen-mile-long flat island with a treacherous coral reef near the British Virgin Islands where hundreds of ships have been wrecked and considerable treasure has been found. The second site described is off the Florida Keys, and the third site is in the Cayman Islands.

The middle section of the book moves from finding treasure to exploring wrecks of ships lost in moments of tragedy. The first account is about the time when Mont Pelée erupted on the island of Martinique and destroyed thirteen ships that were anchored in the Bay of Saint-Pierre. Next is a discussion of ancient shipwrecks in the Mediterranean. This is followed by an account of the ghost fleet of Truck Lagoon, which contains fifty Japanese ships sunk in 1944 and which remains as an underwater park. The quest for the *Titanic* and *Andrea Doria* is described, followed by a discussion of wrecks in harbors nearer home and maritime museums or ship restorations that are open to the public. The final chapter suggests research that is necessary before beginning to locate and dive for treasure.

## Possible Topics for Further Student Investigation

1 This book discusses a variety of areas around the world where interested visitors might visit famous museums or restored ships. Imagine that you are going on a very special vacation. You may visit four of the sites that are of special interest to you. Calculate how far you would travel on your journey. What would you see if you actually got to take such a vacation? Using paper the size of a postcard, make a sketch of something from the museum or some part of a restored ship. Write a message to your class on the back of your "postcard" describing something interesting that you "saw" on your fabulous vacation.

2 This book describes how metal detectors have been used by people near docks and along beaches and reefs to locate treasure. How does a metal detector work? Who in your community would have one? Learn more about metal detectors so that you can explain their workings to your class. Invite someone to visit your class and demonstrate how a metal detector works.

3 In this book, the disaster of Mont Pelée's eruption was discussed and was compared to the eruption of Mount Vesuvius in A.D. 79. Read more about volcanic eruptions. What causes them? Where have the most famous eruptions taken place? Choose six famous volcanic eruptions. Make a bulletin board to share information with your class. Mark the six spots on a world map in the middle of your bulletin board. Include a short written report, including interesting facts, about each of the six eruptions.

# Part II
# Animals and Plants
# Living in and Around
# the Sea

# Animals and Plants Living in and Around the Sea

## ◆ Literature Books ◆

📖*The Blue Heron*
Maggie's troubled life is made better when she can retreat to nature

📖*Dragon of the Lost Sea*
A mythical quest over land and water

📖*Why the Whales Came*
Daniel and Garcie try to help the mysterious Birdman save the whales

## ◆ Bridge ◆

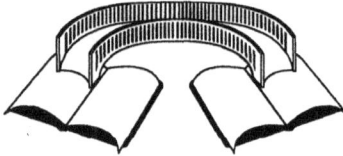

📖*Sevengill, the Shark and Me*
Don Reed tells the life story of a sevengill shark who lives in Marine World

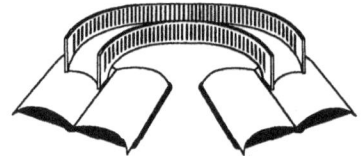

## ◆ Nonfiction Connections ◆

📖*The Horseshoe Crab*
A fascinating look at the life of an amazing sea creature

📖*Life in the Oceans*
What it's really like in the watery world

📖*Meet the Beaver*
A fascinating look at this industrious rodent

📖*Sea Otters*
Saved from extinction, explore the life of this playful animal

📖*Where are My Puffins, Whales, and Seals?*
Explore the balance of life in the world's oceans

📖*Wonders of Sharks*
The title says it all

### OTHER TOPICS TO EXPLORE

—Walrus
—Commercial fishing
—Fish farms
—Dams and flooding
—Sea birds
—Pond waterfowl
—Penguins
—Extinction
—Sport fishing

—Aquariums
—Fly tying
—Myths about sea creatures
—Animal training
—Marine parks
—Whaling laws
—Conservation organizations
—Salt crystals

—Hatcheries
—Adaptation
—Seaweed
—Plankton
—Food chains
—Polar bears
—Seals
—Pearls

# 📖 *Literature Books* 📖

## Animals and Plants Living in and Around the Sea

---

### ◆ Literature Books ◆

📖*The Blue Heron*
Maggie's troubled life is made better when she can retreat to nature

📖*Dragon of the Lost Sea*
A mythical quest over land and water

📖*Why the Whales Came*
Daniel and Garcie try to help the mysterious Birdman save the whales

---

### ◆ Bridge ◆

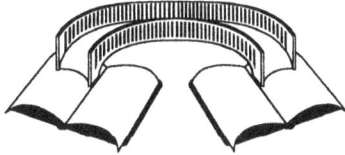

📖*Sevengill, the Shark and Me*
Don Reed tells the life story of a sevengill shark who lives in Marine World

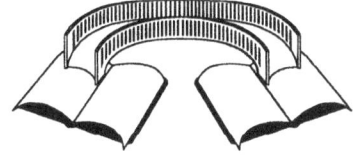

---

### ◆ Nonfiction Connections ◆

📖*The Horseshoe Crab*
A fascinating look at the life of an amazing sea creature

📖*Life in the Oceans*
What it's really like in the watery world

📖*Meet the Beaver*
A fascinating look at this industrious rodent

📖*Sea Otters*
Saved from extinction, explore the life of this playful animal

📖*Where are My Puffins, Whales, and Seals?*
Explore the balance of life in the world's oceans

📖*Wonders of Sharks*
The title says it all

#### OTHER TOPICS TO EXPLORE

—Walrus
—Commercial fishing
—Fish farms
—Dams and flooding
—Sea birds
—Pond waterfowl
—Penguins
—Extinction
—Sport fishing

—Aquariums
—Fly tying
—Myths about sea creatures
—Animal training
—Marine parks
—Whaling laws
—Conservation organizations
—Salt crystals

—Hatcheries
—Adaptation
—Seaweed
—Plankton
—Food chains
—Polar bears
—Seals
—Pearls

# 📖 *The Blue Heron*

by Avi Wortis
New York: Bradbury Press, 1992. 186p.

___

### Type of Book:
This is a realistic, contemporary story, told in the third person from the viewpoint of a girl who is about to turn thirteen.

### Setting:
On the coast of Massachusetts.

### Major Characters:
Margaret Lavcheck, almost thirteen, known as Maggie; her stepmother, Joanna; her father, Alan; and her four-month-old baby half-sister, Linda.

### Other Books by the Author:
*Bright Shadow* (New York: Bradbury Press, 1985), *Captain Grey* (New York: Pantheon Books, 1977), and *Who Was That Masked Man, Anyway?* (New York: Orchard Books, 1992).

## —PLOT SUMMARY—

The viewpoint character, Maggie, is brown-eyed, tall, and about to turn thirteen. Her mother and father have divorced, and Maggie has had to cope with that. One of her fondest hopes is that her father will never change. She talks with him twice a week by phone and always visits him at Christmas.

When the story opens, it is three weeks before Maggie's birthday, and she is living with her mother in Seattle, Washington. Her mother has given her a crystal as an early birthday gift of because Maggie loves things associated with magic and because Maggie will not be in Seattle for her birthday. Maggie is flying back East to spend a month with her father, Alan, his wife of two years, Joanna, and their baby, Linda, who is four months old.

Maggie always spends August with her father. This year she will fly to visit him in Westport, where he has rented a cottage for a month. She lands in Providence, Rhode Island.

When she lands, Maggie's father is not at the airport. Within a few minutes, her stepmother appears, bringing the baby and saying that a last-minute business phone call kept Maggie's father away.

On the drive to the vacation cabin with Joanna, Maggie learns that her father, who is almost fifty, is taking medication for heart palpitations. He has not told Maggie about this, although Joanna thought he had.

Their drive finally takes them to Sawdy Pond and to Finn's Lodge. One of Maggie's first sights is a big blue heron that lives in the marsh behind the cottage.

Maggie phones her mother, who is a nurse practitioner at a community college, to tell her she's arrived safely. That night, the family enjoys a New England dinner of lobster and corn on the cob. She and her father tell knock-knock jokes, but Maggie notices that her father seems snappish.

Maggie sleeps in a loft and feels at home because her fantasy creatures (unicorns, Merlin, Glinda the good witch, a dragon, etc.) from her childhood surround her. She awakes early in the morning, and tiptoes downstairs and out onto the porch. Barefoot, in her nightgown, she goes down the path to the marsh and sees the heron again.

Maggie returns to bed and goes back to sleep. Later, when she gets up, she doesn't tell her father or stepmother about her early morning walk. Her father takes her out in a canoe, but not before he snaps at Joanna for failing to buy groceries. Father and daughter go out into the marsh, and Maggie sees the heron again but does not point it out to her father.

When they get back to the cottage, Maggie's father makes business calls while Maggie baby-sits and Joanna goes shopping for groceries. Then they go to the beach to swim.

Maggie senses that her father is preoccupied. When they get back to the house, her father takes a nap, and Maggie realizes that his unusual behavior has something to do with his illness.

Maggie goes back to the marsh and sees the heron again. She also glimpses something else that frightens the heron away. Maggie is fascinated by the heron's slow, deliberate movements and resolves that it will be her model for the way to act during vacation. She is secretly pleased one day when her father says that Maggie appears to be in slow motion.

Their lives settle into a vacation routine. Joanna reads a lot of child-care books. Her father naps and makes phone calls and works on his business papers. The baby sleeps most of the time.

Maggie sets her alarm for 6:30 a.m. and goes down to look at the heron each day. Usually, she returns to the marsh in the afternoon. Maggie realizes that the small, bush-covered island, with a dead tree standing in the middle, is a place where the heron likes to fish but where something is making the heron uneasy.

One day, when she has failed to see the heron in the morning, Maggie takes the canoe and heads for the island. Exploring it, she finds it is about twenty feet across and is covered with blackberry bushes. The bushes are too thick to walk through, so Maggie goes around the edge of the island.

There she comes upon a tunnel through the bushes. She crawls to the dead tree trunk, where she finds a long box. The box contains comic books, a mug, crackers, peanut butter, an envelope, a radio, and a bow with arrows.

Curious, Maggie opens the envelope from Westport School District, John F. Kennedy School, addressed to Mr. and Mrs. St. Claire from Ms. E. Kirk. The note asks the parents to call and make an appointment regarding their son's behavior. It seems that "Tucker" is still being a bully, provoking fights, and using bad language.

Puzzled by what she's found, Maggie returns to the cottage. She has a headache and goes into the bathroom to get aspirin. There she discovers that her father has three bottles of medicine and that he is not taking any of them. She hears the heron make his worried cry—"frahnk"—and she runs back to the marsh.

The heron is not in sight, but a feather is on the water. Maggie wades out to it and discovers an arrow. She waits until the heron returns, then she breaks the arrow in two and discards it.

That night Joanna takes Maggie for a walk, says how she is ambivalent about all the time that the new baby takes, and confesses how worried she is about Alan. Maggie reveals that she doesn't think her father is taking his medicine, and Joanna asks that she talk to her father about it.

The next morning, Maggie paddles the canoe out into the marsh. Through the mist she thinks she sees another canoe and paddler. She reaches the island and crawls through the tunnel in the blackberry bushes to the box. She can tell from its condition that some other person has been there and gone. She follows a raft around to the other side of the island; from this vantage she sees a house on the coast. Then she leaves.

On Saturday, still not having talked to her father about taking his medicine, Maggie takes the canoe to the island and then to the house. She finds Tucker, age eleven, at home watching TV. He invites Maggie in and explains that his family lives there year-round and that both his parents work on Saturdays. Maggie looks around the small, neat house. She asks Tucker about his family. His mother is a dental hygienist; his father sells floor tile.

Maggie learns that Tucker's sister was killed by a drunk driver when she was twelve and he was only two.

When Maggie asks if Tucker is trying to shoot the heron with an arrow, he responds, "Sure. What's it to you?" Maggie asks him not to kill the heron but realizes that he just doesn't care.

On Sunday, Joanna, Linda, and Maggie go to the Congregational church. Tucker is in church, and he winks at Maggie. Maggie sees his father hit Tucker sharply in the face. After the service, Maggie watches as Tucker leaves, staring straight ahead in the back seat of the car.

On Monday night, Maggie goes out to a movie with her father. They buy popcorn. In the lobby, she sees Tucker and his mother. Tucker calls her "Big Bird." As they leave the theater, Alan asks if Maggie is still interested in magic. She says yes.

At a restaurant after the movie, Maggie asks about the unused medicine. Alan gets angry, jumps up, knocks over the table, and rushes out. Maggie follows.

In the car, Alan speeds away. They are stopped by a police officer and ticketed. They've almost reached home before Alan stops the car and tells Maggie he's afraid. He is worried that his new marriage and the baby are mistakes, and he tells her he's been fired from his job.

When Maggie tries to tell her father how much she loves him, he gets enraged and reminds her that she chose to live with her mother. He forces her out of the car and drives away.

Back at the cottage, Maggie goes inside and tells Joanna what has happened. In the early hours of the morning, the phone rings. They learn that Alan has had a heart attack and run the car off the road. He has a broken arm and broken ribs, black eyes, bruises, and possible internal injuries.

A car comes to take Joanna and the baby to the hospital, but the officials say Maggie is too young to come visit. Left at the cottage alone, Maggie goes back to the marsh. When she sees the heron, she thinks that if the heron dies, her father will die. For Maggie, the heron has become a symbol: if she can touch it, everything will be all right.

Maggie wades out and touches the heron. Then she crawls into Tucker's hiding place on the island and falls asleep. He comes, and she tells him what is happening. She touches him, too, and asks him not to kill the blue heron.

Maggie is allowed a five-minute visit at the hospital to see her father. She helps her stepmother close the vacation cottage, and Maggie prepares to fly back to Seattle. Before she leaves, Maggie makes one more trip to the marsh. She sees the broken bow and arrows. Maggie wades to the island and leaves her special crystal for Tucker. Then the heron comes back, and Maggie sees it one last time.

# 📖 Discussion Starters 📖

*The Blue Heron*
by Avi Wortis

**1** Maggie is interested in magic. One of the main uses she sees for magic is to prevent change from occurring. Why is Maggie so afraid of change?

**2** The first morning of her vacation at the cottage, Maggie creeps out and goes down to see the blue heron. Then she comes back and gets into bed. She doesn't share information about her early morning walk with her father or her stepmother. Why not?

**3** Fascinated by the heron, Maggie uses it as a model for her own movements and is pleased when her father notices that Maggie seems to be moving in slow motion. What does this copying of the heron's slow, deliberate movements have to do with the theme of the book?

**4** When Maggie comes upon Tucker's box near the trunk of the dead tree, she is curious and opens it. For the sake of the plot, it is important that the envelope and note be there, but the other items in the box are there to reveal something about Tucker's character. What are the other items, and what do you learn from them?

**5** Maggie learns that her father is not taking his medicine. She doesn't mention this to him for a few days, and when she finally does, he becomes violently angry. Would there have been a better time for Maggie to discuss the medicine? Why does her father become so angry? Should Joanna have been the one to discuss this with her husband? Why or why not?

**6** What is the significance of Maggie wading out into the water, finding an arrow, and breaking it?

**7** The characters in this book are very ambivalent. Alan questions whether he should have remarried and had another child. Joanna loves the baby but resents the time it takes. Is this ambivalence important to the book? Why?

**8** What is the significance to the story that Tucker's sister was killed by a drunk driver?

**9** Tucker is accused in the note of being a bully. Tucker's father is shown hitting him in church. Discuss and explain what you think might be the relationship between these events.

**10** Why does Maggie leave her precious crystal for Tucker? What significance does it have for her, and why would she think it might be appropriate for Tucker?

## 📖 **Multidisciplinary Activities** 📖

*The Blue Heron*
by Avi Wortis

**1** In this story, Maggie retrieves a feather of the heron that is floating on the water. Studying what makes things float or sink can be quite interesting. Some small objects sink while some large objects float. Do some experiments related to bouyancy. For example, a lemon will float in water even though it's fairly large, but if you peel it, the lemon will sink. Why? Isn't it lighter now? After you have conducted some experiments, you might create a "sink or float" guessing game for members of your class. List the names of several objects. Have students try to place them in the categories of "sink" or "float." Can you come up with some objects that will fool a good portion of your class?

**2** The story closes with a lot of questions left unanswered. Suppose you were writing a sequel to *Blue Heron*. Write the first chapter of the sequel. What will the reader learn about Alan, Joanna, Linda, Tucker, and Maggie? Where will the story be set? Why did you make these choices?

**3** A blue heron is a particularly beautiful bird, one of many varieties of heron. Such things as size; color of plumage; color of beak, legs, and feet; crests; and habitat help a bird-watcher distinguish one variety of heron from another. Learn what you can about herons. Make a drawing (or find pictures) of several different kinds. On a map of the United States, use different shadings or symbols to show where each of the herons might be found.

# 📖 Dragon of the Lost Sea

by Laurence Yep
New York: HarperCollins, 1982. 213p.

**Type of Book:**
This book is a fantasy combining myth, folklore, and a quest. It is told in the first person by a young boy, Thorn, and by a dragon princess, Shimmer.

**Setting:**
A mythical kingdom.

**Major Characters:**
Shimmer, a dragon princess who can assume human form; Thorn, an orphan servant-boy who joins Shimmer on her quest; and Civet, a sorceress.

**Other Books by the Author:**
*Dragon Cauldron* (New York: HarperCollins, 1991), *Dragon Steel* (New York: Harper & Row, 1985), and *Dragon's Gate* (New York: HarperCollins, 1993).

## —PLOT SUMMARY—

The story begins when Shimmer, disguised as a ragged old woman, approaches the town of Amity. She smells magic tinged with the faint scent of the sea on porters and a guard near an inn. Shimmer thinks her enemy, Civet, may be near.

Long ago, Civet stole the entire sea of Shimmer's clan and encapsulated it into an object the size of a pebble. Civet then retreated inside Weeping Mountain. Now all of Shimmer's clan members are forced to be wanderers and beggars in other kingdoms.

By the well, Shimmer finds a ragged, thirteen-year-old servant-boy named Thorn. He is an orphan who works at the inn. A woman and several children at the well are making fun of Thorn because he says he saw a unicorn.

Shimmer is teased when she supports the boy's claim. Thorn throws a bucket of water at the hecklers and then is led by the woman to his master, Knobby, to be punished. Thorn is beaten. Shimmer waits in the kitchen and asks why he defended her.

Thorn says that other than Shimmer, only the woman called "the Widow," who is visiting at the inn, believes that he really saw the unicorn. He says the Widow, who wears a pebble around her neck, is on her way to Edgewood. Shimmer conceals her excitement, but she is certain that the Widow is Civet.

Shimmer knows that Edgewood, 300 kilometers to the southeast, is the nearest human village to the Keeper, a wicked old wizard. Shimmer stays for a dinner of leftovers.

That night, everyone flocks to the inn to hear what the Widow has to say. She tells of many disturbances in the land. Shimmer stays the night at Thorn's request. During the night, Civet sends one of her creatures to kill Thorn. Shimmer attacks him, Thorn sounds the alarm, and Knobby comes with his bow. But before he can use it, the attacker turns into a paper warrior.

Similarly, Civet's other servants have magically changed into paper dolls. Knobby then tries to attack Shimmer. Thorn protects her, and in turn, Shimmer protects Thorn and ends up hitting Knobby with her staff. Knowing that she cannot leave Thorn behind, Shimmer urges him to leave with her.

The two scramble over the village wall. Thorn suspects that Shimmer is a witch. She stops and changes shape by pressing her hand against her forehead, where her magic pearl is hidden. Quickly she assumes her royal dragon princess shape.

The townspeople run toward them, and Shimmer flies off with Thorn on her back. As they fly, Shimmer explains that Civet is the wife of a river spirit. Civet destroyed the river spirit and took over his spells. Shimmer wants to know where to drop Thorn, but he is reluctant to leave her.

Shimmer says the Keeper was a real wizard many years ago until he gave up most of his magic when his servants rebelled and killed many of his strange pets. The Keeper has a mist stone and can change himself into a cloud. He hides in a tower. Thorn insists on accompanying Shimmer.

When they land, Shimmer changes herself into a pilgrim and changes Thorn into a thin, bowlegged man. They walk through a magical forest to the center of the Keeper's old city, creeping between strange trees and mosses. Spiderlike creatures appear. They come to a circle around the Keeper's tower, where they are surrounded by the Keeper's creatures. There's no turning back.

The tower opens, and a thin, old man steps out. He plans to feed Shimmer and Thorn to his pets, so Shimmer turns herself back into her true shape. The Keeper tells Shimmer and Thorn that Civet has already come and stolen his mist stone and is now planning to destroy a city called River Glen. To protect her magic pearl, Shimmer strikes at the Keeper and fights off his creatures.

With Thorn on her back, Shimmer flies away. The Keeper, on the back of a wasp-winged creature, follows them over the Desolate Mountains. When they get over the floor of the dry Lost Sea, they are met by the creatures that the Keeper has sent after Civet. Then the Keeper catches up with them. Surrounded, Thorn and Shimmer fight for their lives.

The Keeper then pretends to try to strike a deal with Shimmer to join forces and go after Civet. But while he talks, he works a spell. A giant net of fire forms. Shimmer escapes it. The net captures the Keeper and his pets, who all fall to the floor of the Lost Sea.

Shimmer lands with a jolt. She has been injured during the battle. Thorn realizes that Shimmer, who is only a child dragon, does not fully know how to use her magic. He also recognizes that if Shimmer catches Civet, she will not only recover her lost kingdom but also clear up the misunderstanding about the pearl that led to her banishment for stealing it from her brother.

Thorn and Shimmer see a mound in the sea that Shimmer says was once her grandfather's beautiful coral palace. Because of her wounds, Shimmer cannot fly, so they set off on foot. For several days they walk across the salt-crusted sea floor with winds blowing salt in their faces. Thorn grows so weak that Shimmer has to carry him. When Shimmer is temporarily blinded by the glare of the salt, Thorn suggests that she turn herself into a cat so that he can carry her. Shimmer reluctantly agrees.

Thorn builds a warm fire, and Shimmer catches some lizards, which they eat. Feeling better, Shimmer becomes a dragon again, and they follow a dry river route through a canyon. They reach what used to be a large lake and go on through a mountain pass to River Glen. Shimmer's wing has healed sufficiently so that she is able to kill a mountain goat, which they eat. They get water from the springs along the route.

They finally see a large valley and find the town of River Glen, which is very run-down. Shimmer changes into the form of a merchant and changes Thorn into a servant. They are met at the town gate by guards who have been appointed by the Great Sage.

Shimmer recognizes the Great Sage. In the past, he was a trouble-maker named Monkey, who forced Shimmer's uncle to give him a magic rod. Monkey tried to set up his own kingdom but was stopped by a kindly wizard named Old Boy, who put a circlet around Monkey's head. When Monkey disobeys Old Boy, Monkey's head hurts terribly. Shimmer recognizes the guard as Monkey in disguise. Monkey explains that he is there to guard against Civet.

Monkey and Shimmer get into an argument but, at Thorn's suggestion, finally go inside to continue their conversation in private. Monkey confesses that all the local inhabitants have left and that he magically made pretend people from the hairs in his tail. Monkey drugs Shimmer and Thorn because he himself wants to capture Civet and claim all the glory.

Thorn wakes first and tries to awaken Shimmer. Civet arrives and tricks Monkey. She releases the waters she has captured and floods the city. Shimmer must decide whether to go after Civet or rescue Thorn. She rescues Thorn, and from the top of the tower they see Monkey and Civet wrestling in the sea. Civet uses the mist stone to turn into a cloud and escape.

Monkey puzzles about how to remove the sea from River Glen but confesses that he doesn't know the whereabouts of his master, Old Boy, who might have enough magic to do it. Monkey decides to try to use a cauldron to boil away the sea, because that is less dangerous than going after Civet.

When Monkey realizes that Shimmer and Thorn are going on to Weeping Mountain, he gives Thorn a hair to wear like a ring. On command, the hair will magically turn into a chain that will hold even Civet. On their way to the mountain, Shimmer and Thorn stop to cut some reeds for torches.

When they get close to Civet's castle, Shimmer and Thorn use torches to explore the caverns of Weeping Mountain. They are attacked by tigers, which turn to paper when touched with fire.

As they continue, a crossbow bolt is shot into Shimmer. Thorn proves himself to be an able ally. Wounded, and with a shortage of torches, they continue. Five swordswomen block their way. Again, fighting with the torches, Shimmer and Thorn emerge victorious.

They continue into a room filled with pools. In the image of a sixteen-year-old girl, Civet appears. She uses the power of water and earth to capture Thorn and Shimmer. They are bound by tree roots. Thorn pretends to want to serve Civet as a cook and thereby manages to save his life.

Civet tells how the King Within the River had spied her long ago and wanted her for his bride. She blames her father and people for dropping her into the river to drown and live with the ugly King.

Thorn prepares a bowl of noodles for Civet. She insists that he eat some before she does. Thorn reluctantly obliges. While she waits to see if he has been poisoned, Civet tells about her life with the King Within the River, how she learned his magic, and how she finally destroyed him by turning him into stone.

Seeing that Thorn is still alive, Civet begins to eat. She swallows the Monkey's hair that Thorn has hidden in the noodles. Immediately Thorn yells, "Change!" The hair became a strong chain that binds Civet. Thorn takes the mist stone and rescues Shimmer, who offers to spare Civet if she will return the stolen sea. Civet says she and her magic are too weak to do so.

As the story ends, Shimmer adopts Thorn. They set off to find a powerful magician in the dragon kingdom who, with Civet's help, may be able to create new spells. They leave hoping that the High King of the Dragons might cancel the decree that made Shimmer an outlaw.

## 📖 Discussion Starters 📖

### Dragon of the Lost Sea
### by Laurence Yep

**1** In a successful fantasy, there are enough real and human elements so that the reader feels comfortable accepting the unreal and fantastic elements. Choose a section of the story and point out what elements are familiar and real and what elements are fantastic. Explain how these work together to capture the reader's imagination.

**2** Shimmer has a magic pearl. Civet wears a magic pebble around her neck. The Keeper has a mist stone. Each of these stones represents power and magic. Which is the more powerful "charm"? Why do you think this?

**3** Some books are told from one point of view only, and others are told from multiple points of view. *Dragon of the Lost Sea* is mostly told from the viewpoint of Shimmer, the dragon. But two of the chapters are told from the viewpoint of Thorn, the human. Why do you think the author decided to use the viewpoint of Thorn for two of the twenty chapters? What special effect does the shift in viewpoint have?

**4** Monkey is a strange creature. He has both good points and bad points. What are his character defects? What are his positive attributes? On the whole, do you like or dislike Monkey? Why?

**5** A young boy appears puny beside a dragon, yet Thorn holds his own in several situations. Find at least two instances in the story where you can show that the human is responsible for saving the dragon.

**6** The author includes at least two instances where the reader is given reason to question who Thorn, the orphan, might be. The innkeeper, Knobby, tells a story about a queen and her son who vanished. Could Thorn be a prince? Later in the story, Monkey says, "I've seen your face before, boy." Does Monkey remember him because he is royalty? Neither of these instances is developed in the book. Why do you think they are there? Did you have questions about Thorn? Who do you think he is? Do you think that the author intends to take up this thread of the story in a sequel?

**7** Throughout the book, whenever Civet's magic falters, her various "creatures" turn into paper dolls. What is the significance of this?

**8** Trees are used in many different ways in the story. Those around the Keeper's castle are menacing and have humanlike features. Some plants in the caverns have turned to stone. Civet uses trees to capture Shimmer and Thorn. Consider the use of trees throughout the book. What is their importance? Are they used as a symbol for some quality? If so, what?

**9** Shimmer is hurt frequently throughout the story. Injuries sometimes prevent her from flying, and her inability to fly leads the story in a different direction, with Shimmer becoming a clumsy foot traveler. Why do you think that a magical creature like Shimmer cannot heal herself? Is this a weakness or a strength of Shimmer?

**10** Although the story ends, it doesn't feel as if it's entirely over because the Lost Sea isn't restored, and there are other unresolved issues. What do you think happens next? How is Shimmer received by the High King of the Dragons? Who does Thorn turn out to be?

# 📖 **Multidisciplinary Activities** 📖

## *Dragon of the Lost Sea*
### by Laurence Yep

**1** Many places in this magical kingdom have interesting names: Weeping Mountain, Desolate Mountains, Edgewood, River Glen, Lost Sea. Design a mythical island of approximately 1,000 square miles. Make a scale model of your island. Include rivers, mountains, and lakes as well as cities and ports. Give each a name. Use a map legend to indicate size of towns, railroads, or other features.

**2** During several days of the story, Thorn and Shimmer walk across the salt beds in their mythical kingdom. Where are there salt beds in the real world? Do they have any commercial value? Find out about these and report on them to your class.

**3** Strange trees play major roles throughout this story. You can create a rather strange tree of your own. You will need: four pipe cleaners, a paper coffee-maker filter, a narrow-necked jar, a wooden stick, a pencil, a small funnel, cotton thread, a pair of tin snips, 250 grams of copper sulphate, and 200 milliliters of water in a saucepan.

Cut four pipe cleaners in half. Take four of the pieces and twist them together to form the trunk of a tree. Twist the other four pieces, one by one, around the trunk, and shape them to look like tree limbs. Clip the limbs with the tin snips to shape your tree so that it looks like a pine tree, with shorter limbs near the top and longer ones near the bottom. Tie a piece of thread to the tree trunk.

Heat the water until it boils and then allow it to cool a little. Pour it into a narrow-necked jar. Add the copper sulphate a little at a time, stirring it with the wooden stick, until no more will dissolve. Put your coffee-maker filter into the funnel so undissolved particles will be caught. Slowly pour the copper sulphate solution through the funnel into the jar. Place the jar in a sunny window sill. Tie the end of the short thread that is attached to your tree to the middle of a pencil. Balance the pencil across the top of the jar so that your pipe-cleaner tree hangs in the solution.

As the water evaporates, crystals will grow on your tree. When your model is crystallized, carefully remove it from the jar. Treat it gently so that the crystals do not break off.

**Note**—Copper sulphate is poisonous. Do not eat the crystals that form. Be sure to clean up carefully and thoroughly.

# 📖 *Why the Whales Came*

by Michael Morpurgo
New York: Scholastic, 1985. 139p.

**Type of Book:**
This is a realistic story set during the First World War and told in the first person by ten-year-old Gracie Jenkins.

**Setting:**
The story is set on the Isles of Scilla, tiny islands in the Atlantic Ocean near England.

**Major Characters:**
Gracie Jenkins; her mother, Clemmie; her father; Daniel Pender, a friend; and the Birdman of Bryher.

**Other Books by the Author:**
*King of the Cloud Forests* (New York: Viking Kestrel, 1988), *Mr. Nobody's Eyes* (New York: Viking Kestrel, 1990), and *Waiting for Anya* (New York: Viking, 1991).

## —PLOT SUMMARY—

Gracie Jenkins and Daniel Pender were warned to stay away from the Birdman of Bryher. People think he's mad. The Birdman goes barefoot in winter, wears a black sou'wester and cape, and walks with a limp. Seagulls fly above him, and a kittiwake sits on his shoulder. He has a black-jack donkey and a great woolly dog.

But the children like to sail a fleet of boats they have made, and it seems that Rushy Bay, which is forbidden territory, is the only safe place to sail them. So even though Gracie is afraid, she and Daniel go up on Samson Hill to sail two boats, *Shag* and *Turnstone*, in Rushy Bay. At lunchtime, they leave their boats, and when they return after lunch, the boats are gone.

They find them, along with a boat they'd lost earlier, the *Cormorant*, resting on the beach. Nearby, the initials *Z* and *W* are written in the sand with orange shells. They hear a donkey bray, and the two children flee.

That night, Gracie's father tells her that the Birdman's mother was named Woodcock and that she's been dead for thirty years. When he was a boy, Gracie's father dared Charlie Webber to go to Samson Island, the Ghost Island. Charlie took the dare. That night, Charlie's house burned down, then Charlie caught scarlet fever (which almost every child on the island caught). Charlie told Gracie's father that the Birdman had come to him and said he was sorry, but there was nothing he could do to erase the curse of Samson.

The Birdman explained to Charlie that, when he was a boy, the people in his town found a ghost ship run aground. The men rowed out, found no one on board, and sailed it to Penzance to claim salvage money. The ship foundered, and all the men drowned. Finally, everyone left the island except for the Birdman and his mother.

Although Gracie's parents warn her to keep away, a few days later she goes to Rushy Bay again with Daniel. They find a carved cormorant where their boats had been. Spelled on the sand in addition to the initials *Z* and *W* is a message: "Stay

and play. Your beach as much as mine."
The two children play. When they go
home, Gracie hides the cormorant.

They decide to make a gift for the
Birdman, a boat named *Woodcock*. They
take it to Rushy Bay and leave it for the
Birdman along with a message. The next
day when they return, there is a message.
"Thanks. Beautiful. Zachariah Woodcock."

Gracie resents going to school in summer because it interferes with her playing,
but after school and chores, the children
go to Rushy Bay. The Birdman continues
to leave them messages in the sand. From
the messages, they learn that the Birdman is eighty years old and that he's
carved birds all his life.

Mr. Angus Wellbeloved, their teacher,
tells them he thinks there will be a war
with Germany. The children share this
news with the Birdman. During August of
1914, Daniel begins carving. At first, he is
none too successful, but he keeps at it.

The children never talk to the Birdman, although they sometimes see him.
One stormy night, everyone goes to a
meeting to talk about the war with Germany. The people decide to post a lookout
for submarines on Watch Hill and to have
a "blackout" on the island at night. Because they know the Birdman often goes
out in bad weather in his boat, the children are more concerned about the storm
than they are about the start of the war.

The next day, Gracie and Daniel
hurry to see if the Birdman is all right.
They find no message on the beach, and
fearing he may be in trouble, the children
go to the cottage. The Birdman isn't there,
but they go inside and see his hundreds of
carvings and the bread that he has baked.
They are about to leave when the Birdman
appears. He tells them that he had to
spend the night on Samson Island because
of the storm.

The Birdman explains that he is deaf,
a result of a fever when he was a child. He
tells them that some good timber has
washed up on shore from the storm and
that they should tell their families to go
get it. He gives them another carving.

The islanders scramble to get the
wood before the Preventative (Customs)
officers come and claim it. When the Pre-

ventatives come, they search each house
for the timbers. During the search, the
cormorant that Gracie has hidden is found
and the searchers are curious about it.
Gracie's father pretends that his grandfather carved it, but later, he angrily asks
Gracie about it. Gracie says Daniel carved
it and that it was going to be a surprise
Christmas present. Father believes that
Daniel carved the cormorant, but Mother
is suspicious.

Gracie and Daniel continue to visit
the Birdman. Gracie kneads dough and
tries to milk the goats. They invent a secret
sign language. In time, the Birdman is
able to read their lips. Daniel spends a lot
of time learning to carve from the Birdman, who wants to pass on his skills.

The only time the Birdman becomes
angry is when Daniel asks him about
ghosts on Samson Island. The Birdman
says there are ghosts there, but you can't
see them. He tells them that the souls of
the guilty men of Samson Island will be
there until he can free them.

Then one day, Gracie's father announces that he's joined the navy. Mother
now has to do her housework and Father's
work as well. She becomes ill from over-
working. Gracie usually can't go with
Daniel now to see the Birdman because
she has too many chores to do.

The Birdman often leaves gifts on
their doorstep: honey, bread, eggs, pota-
toes, or milk. Mother doesn't know who
leaves these things, but Gracie does.
Father's money isn't enough with winter
coming on. Gracie wants to go out fishing
with Daniel, but her mother won't hear of
it.

One day Gracie and Daniel set off in
a fishing boat. They catch some fish, but
the fog comes in quickly and they are soon
lost. They try to row home but go off
course. In the dark, they see a speck of
light and row to an island. It is Samson
Island, and Daniel thinks the Birdman is
the one who lighted the fire there.

They search many roofless, empty cot-
tages and then come upon one that the
Birdman has stayed in. It has a roof and
two cots. There's also a gigantic, unicorn-
like horn above the fireplace. They find a
well, but it's dry. They eat their fish in the

cottage, and when the fog lifts, they head for home.

When they arrive home, they're met at the beach. Gracie's mother is kind to her, but Daniel's father promises him a beating for taking the boat without permission and having everyone on the island out searching for them.

One day at school, Daniel's brother, Big Tim, and ten other kids surround Daniel and call him a Hun-lover for having visited the Birdman. They say that the Birdman's hut is the only one that doesn't observe the blackouts. Tim says he'll tell his father and that officials will come and investigate and maybe shoot the Birdman.

Gracie doesn't understand why Daniel has told her that he hasn't been to see the Birdman when in fact he has. That afternoon, when Gracie gets home there is a message that her father is missing. She feels a curse has come upon them because of her visit to Samson Island. People come with flowers and jam and hushed voices. Then the Birdman comes and says he's sorry and leaves a pot of honey.

Big Tim tells his father all about Daniel and the Birdman, and the police come and search the Birdman's cottage. Finding nothing suspicious, they tell Daniel's father not to bother the Birdman again. Daniel's father punishes Big Tim, and Big Tim and his friends plan a dawn attack.

When Daniel and Gracie go to warn the Birdman, they find him at the beach with a narwhal. The Birdman explains that if one of the narwhals is beached, others swim in to join him until they are all beached. In the past, the men of Samson Island slaughtered them and took all the horns but one with them on the "ghost ship" to Penzance.

The Birdman and his mother found one horn left on the beach, half buried in sand, and it is this horn that Gracie saw in the cabin on Samson Island. To keep people off Samson Island, the Birdman rows out there when a fog comes in and lights a beacon to warn away ships.

Daniel, Gracie, and the Birdman can't push or drag the narwhal to the sea. Big Tim and his friends arrive, destroy the henhouse and windows at the Birdman's cabin, and run down to the beach. Instead of helping get the narwhal into the sea, they go to get the townspeople.

The villagers come to slaughter the narwhals. But Gracie's mother tells them how the Birdman has helped her and demands that they listen to his story before they act. Mother galvanizes the people into action to save the narwhal.

Once the narwhal is put back into the water, it joins the others, but they all remain in the bay. Everyone gets pots and pans and makes banging noises to scare away the narwhals. Then the villagers light torches to try to drive away the narwhals.

The Birdman has his breath knocked out by a wave and is brought back on the beach to rest. Finally, scared of the fire, the narwhals leave. Although Gracie's mother asks the Birdman to come home that night with them, he refuses and says he'll go out in the boat to be sure that the narwhals have gone. The next morning, the Birdman is gone, but he has left his dog, Prince, and his initials on the beach.

The next Sunday, there is a special memorial service for Gracie's father and the Birdman. Then for two weeks there are gales, making it too stormy for the boat to take the children to school.

On Monday, the church bells ring out. Gracie and her mother go to the quay. A boat is there from St. Mary's, and Gracie's father is being hauled up on everyone's shoulders. He explains that his ship was torpedoed and he was rescued by a fishing boat. He has shore leave because of his injured leg.

Daniel shouts that the curse is over. All the boats go that afternoon to Samson Island. As Daniel predicts, the well is no longer dry. He, Gracie, and Prince drink from it.

# 📖 **Discussion Starters** 📖

*Why the Whales Came*
by Michael Morpurgo

**1** During the first chapter of the book, you read what many people say about the Birdman: he's mad, he's the devil, he uses spells and curses. The first line of the books says, "You keep away from the Birdman, Gracie." What is the effect that the author produces in this first chapter?

**2** Big Tim, Daniel's brother, appears briefly but frequently throughout the book. What is Big Tim like? What actions and words does the author use to convey Big Tim's personality?

**3** For the teacher, Mr. Angus Wellbeloved, arithmetic is the yardstick by which he judges character. Have you known someone who judged others only by how they measured up in one particular area? What is the effect of such judgment?

**4** The Birdman is lonely and an outcast. Everyone avoids him. He lives all alone except for his animals. Why do you suppose the author adds the burden of deafness to the Birdman? Would the story have been much different if he could hear? What aspects of the story would change?

**5** Because the Birdman can't hear, a person who wants to communicate with him must either mouth words so that he can lip read or write the words on paper. Daniel chooses to talk and let the Birdman read his lips. Gracie chooses to write what she wants to communicate. What character traits of each child account for the difference?

**6** When Daniel and Gracie are on Samson Island looking for water, they come upon a dry well. At the end of the story, when the curse is gone and everyone goes out to Samson Island, they find the well filled with water again. There is a supernatural explanation for this, but could there be a natural explanation? What might it be?

**7** When the narwhal is stranded on the beach and most of the townspeople appear to slaughter it and the other nawhals in the bay, it is Gracie's mother who speaks up and takes charge. What enables her to speak with such authority that the others listen?

**8** At the end of chapter eleven, it is suggested that the Birdman might have left a final message for the children, along with Prince, on the beach, but that the message has accidentally been erased. If you were the Birdman, what final message would you have left written in the sand?

**9** When Gracie's father comes home after everyone thought he was dead, he faces his wife and child. The author could have written this reunion scene in many different ways. He chose to have Gracie's mother say nothing at all, and Gracie's father's first words to his wife are, "Bit late for breakfast, am I, Clemmie?" Is this scene powerful or weak? What makes it so?

**10** Once everyone realizes that the curse has been removed from Samson Island and they go there and look around, you might think that some people would choose to live there. Yet, in the final sentences of the book, you are told that if you visit Samson Island, you'll see ruins and find a well of water, but you'll be alone. What effect does the notion of Samson Island still being empty produce on you as a reader? Is it an effective way to conclude the book? Why or why not?

## 📖 **Multidisciplinary Activities** 📖

*Why the Whales Came*
by Michael Morpurgo

**1** A narwhal is a very strange creature. Do some research. Where are narwhals found? For what purpose is their horn used? Do they have any commercial value? What is their major enemy? What do they eat? Share the information in a written report.

**2** The townspeople meet and decide to have a "blackout" each night. Blackouts and "dimouts" were also common in the Second World War in communities throughout the United States. These were enforced by "civilian air raid wardens" who patrolled neighborhoods for this purpose. Do some research into the Second World War. Find out more about blackouts and dimouts, particularly those along coasts. What was the purpose of the blackout and of the dimout? How effective were they? Share what you learn in an oral report to your class.

**3** The Birdman has been a wood-carver all his life. His birds are especially beautiful. If you are interested in wood carving, try carving a sea bird or animal and bring it in to share with your class. What sort of tools did you use? What kinds of wood are best for carving and why? If there is a professional wood-carver in your town, invite him or her to come to your class and share carvings and techniques.

# 📖 *Bridge* 📖

## Animals and Plants Living in and Around the Sea

### ◆ Literature Books ◆

📖*The Blue Heron*
Maggie's troubled life is made better when she can retreat to nature

📖*Dragon of the Lost Sea*
A mythical quest over land and water

📖*Why the Whales Came*
Daniel and Garcie try to help the mysterious Birdman save the whales

### ◆ Bridge ◆

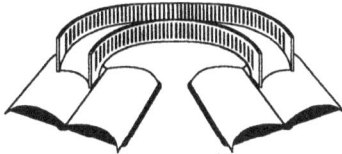

📖*Sevengill, the Shark and Me*
Don Reed tells the life story of a sevengill shark who lives in Marine World

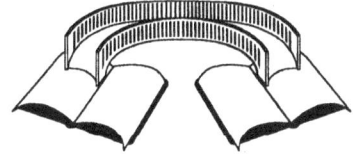

### ◆ Nonfiction Connections ◆

📖*The Horseshoe Crab*
A fascinating look at the life of an amazing sea creature

📖*Life in the Oceans*
What it's really like in the watery world

📖*Meet the Beaver*
A fascinating look at this industrious rodent

📖*Sea Otters*
Saved from extinction, explore the life of this playful animal

📖*Where are My Puffins, Whales, and Seals?*
Explore the balance of life in the world's oceans

📖*Wonders of Sharks*
The title says it all

#### OTHER TOPICS TO EXPLORE

—Walrus
—Commercial fishing
—Fish farms
—Dams and flooding
—Sea birds
—Pond waterfowl
—Penguins
—Extinction
—Sport fishing

—Aquariums
—Fly tying
—Myths about sea creatures
—Animal training
—Marine parks
—Whaling laws
—Conservation organizations
—Salt crystals

—Hatcheries
—Adaptation
—Seaweed
—Plankton
—Food chains
—Polar bears
—Seals
—Pearls

# 📖 *Sevengill, the Shark and Me*

by Don C. Reed
New York: Alfred A. Knopf, 1986. 126p.

This is a full-length, true-life adventure book that is mostly text, with a few black-and-white illustrations. This volume, a Sierra Club book, represents part of the organization's publishing program, which supports books that encourage the public to protect the earth's scenic and ecological resources.

The author, Don C. Reed, was head diver at California's Marine World/Africa U.S.A. At the time that he wrote this book, he had spent approximately 12,000 hours underwater. In addition to this book, he has written an adult book, *Notes from an Underwater Zoo*, and has also written a number of magazine articles, both for children and for adults.

Reed gives information about the broadhead sevengilled sharks by discussing in detail one massive female shark named Sevengill. This book makes an excellent bridge from fiction to nonfiction because Reed reconstructs the shark's birth and early life from what he has learned about other sharks; this short portion is fictitious.

Then Reed gives a factual report of Sevengill's life and his experiences with her, beginning with the time she was first caught. He tells about how she was transported to live in San Francisco's Steinhart Aquarium and how she was moved to Marine World. Using personal anecdotes, he explains that every dive into a shark tank has the potential to become dangerous.

## Possible Topics for Further Student Investigation

1. Few creatures have a reputation as bad as the shark's. The reader learns that baby sharks are often the victims of a number of creatures that threaten them. In this book, these enemies include a mud shark, a diving cormorant, a striped bass, and three sea lions. Do some additional research on different types of sharks. On what animals do they prey? What other predators are dangerous to the shark? Write a short paper and share your findings with your class.

2. Sevengill sharks have strange pin-sized holes on their snouts. These holes are called Ampullae of Lorenzini, and they are used to help sharks navigate. Each pinhole holds a jellylike substance and a single hair. Much like you might use a compass, the shark is able to use Ampullae of Lorenzini to sense magnetic currents. Research the ways that sharks navigate. Share your findings in an oral report to your class.

3. There are a number of famous aquariums throughout the United States. These aquariums can be a rich resource for student investigation. Are there any large aquariums close to you? If so, try to arrange a visit? Be sure to write down any questions you have before your field trip. If you have specific questions and cannot visit an aquarium, write to an aquarium for information, being sure to include a stamped, self-addressed envelope so that you get a response. One aquarium you can write to is the National Aquarium in Baltimore, Pier 3, 501 E. Pratt Street, Baltimore, MD 21233.

# 📖 *Nonfiction Connections* 📖

## Animals and Plants Living in and Around the Sea

---

### ◆ Literature Books ◆

📖*The Blue Heron*
Maggie's troubled life is made better when she can retreat to nature

📖*Dragon of the Lost Sea*
A mythical quest over land and water

📖*Why the Whales Came*
Daniel and Garcie try to help the mysterious Birdman save the whales

---

### ◆ Bridge ◆

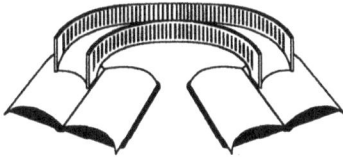

📖*Sevengill, the Shark and Me*
Don Reed tells the life story of a sevengill shark who lives in Marine World

---

### ◆ Nonfiction Connections ◆

📖*The Horseshoe Crab*
A fascinating look at the life of an amazing sea creature

📖*Life in the Oceans*
What it's really like in the watery world

📖*Meet the Beaver*
A fascinating look at this industrious rodent

📖*Sea Otters*
Saved from extinction, explore the life of this playful animal

📖*Where are My Puffins, Whales, and Seals?*
Explore the balance of life in the world's oceans

📖*Wonders of Sharks*
The title says it all

#### OTHER TOPICS TO EXPLORE

—Walrus
—Commercial fishing
—Fish farms
—Dams and flooding
—Sea birds
—Pond waterfowl
—Penguins
—Extinction
—Sport fishing

—Aquariums
—Fly tying
—Myths about sea creatures
—Animal training
—Marine parks
—Whaling laws
—Conservation organizations
—Salt crystals

—Hatcheries
—Adaptation
—Seaweed
—Plankton
—Food chains
—Polar bears
—Seals
—Pearls

# 📖 *The Horseshoe Crab*

by Nancy Day
New York: Dillon Press, 1992. 60p.

This is a short, five-chapter book that describes, through text and color photographs, the physical characteristics, habits, and life cycle of the horseshoe crab and its importance to medical research.

The reader learns a variety of interesting facts about *Limulus polyphemus*, the horseshoe crab, such as that it grows to a length of twenty-four inches, sometimes swims upside down, and has a life span of fifteen to twenty years.

The horseshoe crab that can be found on the beach today is almost identical to the ones that lived during the time of the dinosaurs, so in many respects the horseshoe crab can be thought of as a living fossil with ancestors that go back 500 million years.

Of medical importance are the crab's unusual eyes, which have helped researchers understand eyesight and win a 1967 Nobel Prize in the process. Also important are the special design of its heart and its blood, which turns blue when it is exposed to air. This processed blood is worth as much as $15,000 a quart. Drug manufacturers use the horseshoe crab blood to test whether or not drugs are pure enough to be injected into humans. They can also use the processed horseshoe crab blood to detect unusual infections in people and animals.

## Possible Topics for Further Student Investigation

**1** The billions of eggs that horseshoe crabs lay on beaches along the East Coast of the United States are crucial to sustain the millions of shore birds on their way to nesting areas near the Arctic Circle. Find out more about this annual bird migration. Which types of birds are involved? What routes do they fly? Share your findings orally or in a written report to your class.

**2** The Japanese horseshoe crab has become endangered. Find out more about the three species of horseshoe crabs that are found around Japan, India, and Indonesia. Why are these dying out? Is there a danger to *Limulus polyphemus*, the species that lives along the East Coast of the United States? What poses a danger? Use world maps to show members of your class where the different species of horseshoe crabs live, and indicate which of these are endangered.

**3** In the 1870s, many people thought of horseshoe crabs as pests and were killing millions simply to use them for fertilizer. During this time, some cities and towns on Cape Cod put bounties on horseshoe crabs. Use a library to research this period of maritime history. Using statistics that you find, graph the crab population over the years to show what happened in the Delaware Bay area. Also show how the horseshoe crab population, which once was dangerously low, is now making a comeback.

# 📖*Life in the Oceans*

by Norbert Wu
Boston: Little, Brown, 1991. 96p.

This book is an introduction to the many living things in oceans, ranging from microscopic plants to huge whales. Norbert Wu wrote the text and also provided the brilliant color photographs that illustrate the book.

In the section on the open ocean, the reader learns about floating pastures, the food chain, the life of a jellyfish, and the lives of other unusual animals. The second section deals with coral reefs and explains why they are in peril.

The kelp forests of the ocean grow up from depths of 100 feet and have creatures living among them that in many ways are as diverse as those in a tropical rain forest.

These forests grow in the cold waters off the west coasts of North and South America and the southern coasts of Australia, New Zealand, and South Africa.

A chapter on the deep ocean is the result of travel in a small submersible, a steel tube, in which the author/photographer was the only passenger. He rode on his stomach and looked out four thick windows into the oceans' depths.

The final section of the book tries to look into the future, recognizing that oil spills, toxic wastes, unsupervised large-scale fishing, and other factors threaten the oceans of the world and the creatures that live in or near them.

## Possible Topics for Further Student Investigation

1  Part of the appeal of this book is found in its dramatic photographs, taken underwater. If you are interested in photography, you might want to find out more about underwater photography. What sort of camera is needed? Is special film used? How can light be maximized? Are there special procedures for developing? If possible, ask someone in your community who is familiar with underwater photography to visit the class, explain techniques, show equipment, and share color slides.

2  Bioluminescent light is an interesting topic about which many books and articles have been written. This light is particularly important to various fish that live in the deep ocean. It is thought that the luminous organs may attract prey. Research this topic. Then prepare a paper and use it to orally share your information with classmates. If possible, bring in some pictures from magazines or books to illustrate your talk.

3  Few people can resist picking up a beautiful shell at the beach. It may be a large conch or abalone or a tiny, colorful spiral. Someone in your community is certain to have an extensive shell collection and knowledge about the various creatures that once lived in these shells. When you have located your resource person, invite him or her to visit your class and bring in the collection of shells to share and discuss.

# 📖 *Meet the Beaver*

## by Leonard Lee Rue III, with William Owen
New York: Dodd, Mead, 1986. 80p.

This book provides an excellent introduction to beavers. It is illustrated with exceptionally fine, black-and-white photographs.

In the first section of the book, the author points out that beavers, like humans, alter their environment to suit their needs. The beaver modifies its world through its dam-building activities.

The beaver's body is built to function smoothly. The book reveals this through detailed photographs as well as text. The reader learns that the beaver's flat tail can be used to sound a warning signal, its fur is almost waterproof, its eyelids are transparent, its forefeet are as flexible as a human hand, and its hind feet are webbed.

Other sections of the book describe where to find beavers, how they use their senses and communicate, how they move on land and in water, what they eat, how they give birth and care for their young, how they behave during the different seasons of the year, and how beavers interact with humans. The enemies of the beaver are also described.

The author traces how Native Americans trapped the beaver for food and fur; how fur-trading companies, such as the Hudson Bay Company, diminished the beaver population; and how the beaver population has made a comeback.

## Possible Topics for Further Student Investigation

**1** A beaver is a rodent. It has the large front incisor teeth, used for gnawing, that are characteristic of all rodents. Draw or find pictures of at least six rodents. Concentrate on showing the teeth of the animal. Display your set of pictures with identifying captions. Under each rodent's picture, post a short paragraph indicating how this particular rodent uses its gnawing teeth.

**2** A common phrase is the expression "busy as a beaver." Other creatures are also characterized by phrases, such as "hungry as a bear," "sly as a fox," and "slow as a turtle." Think about a number of animals and the characteristics we associate with them. Write and illustrate a short picture book using these expressions, or original ones that you make up, that you might share with a kindergarten class.

**3** Beaver fur was so valued by Europeans that the beaver population was almost wiped out by early traders and colonists in the United States. Beaver fur was used for coats and hats. Research this topic. During what years were beaver furs particularly fashionable? What did a beaver hat look like? Find some pictures of these beaver fashions and share them with your class. What furs are particularly valued for fur coats and hats today? How are these furs supplied? Have there been any problems in modern times with the fur industry? What sorts of problems? Report what you learn.

# 📖 *Sea Otters*

by Ruth Ashby
New York: Atheneum, 1990. 32p.

This book is part of the Jane Goodall's Animal World series. It is a short and easy-to-read book that is illustrated mainly with color photographs.

In the first section of the book, a map shows the distribution of the sea otter population. This is followed by a drawing of a family tree illustrating otter evolution. Next, a sea otter community is discussed in detail. The range of individual otters is examined, along with "territories" and the activities of large groups of otters that combine into what is called a "raft."

Sections of the book are devoted to describing how sea otters move in the water and on land, and to describing their specialized senses. There is information about how otters can recognize others by scent and about the variety of sounds that they can make. A sea otter's fur, the thickest of any of the mammals, is described in detail, including its layers and its waterproofing and insulating capabilities. The book also describes how a sea otter grooms its fur.

The book describes the life of young sea otters, their growth, and typical day-to-day activities.

The final section of the book is devoted to information about protecting sea otters from a variety of dangers, including the pollution that results from oil spills.

## Possible Topics for Further Student Investigation

1  A number of interesting facts about sea otters and their near extinction are given in this book. Use these facts to make up interesting math problems for your fellow students to solve. For example, after supplying the necessary information, you might pose these problems:

> What fraction of the sea otters killed in the 170 years before 1911 were killed along the Alaskan coast?

> In 1911, an estimated 50 sea otters were left along the California coast. Today there are 1,864. What percentage increase is that?

2  This book states that sea otters often don't do well in captivity. Are there sea otters in an aquarium or a zoo near you? Write or visit to ask questions about the care of sea otters. How much space do they have? At what temperature is their water kept? What are they fed, and how often? Call ahead to make an appointment if you are going to interview someone. If you are writing, be sure to include a stamped, self-addressed envelope to ensure that you receive a reply. Share what you learn with the class.

3  The author of this book became so interested in sea otters that she formed an organization known as Friends of the Sea Otter. What are its purposes? How many members does it have? Where is its home office located? Are there other organizations like it designed to protect other sea creatures? What are they? Share the information that you gather with interested classmates.

# 📖 *Where Are My Puffins, Whales, and Seals?*

by Ron Hirschi
New York: Bantam Books, 1992. 44p.

---

This National Audubon Society book contains a minimum amount of text and many excellent color photographs. It is part of a series of One Earth books, aimed at helping young people become aware of their responsibilities toward wildlife.

The book discusses the balance of life in the oceans and the fact that many animals that live in the world's waters have been driven to the brink of extinction because of thoughtless human actions and because of the shortsighted overharvesting of sea creatures.

The book describes the extinction and the threat of extinction of some popula-tions, including the Atlantic and western Pacific gray whales. It also points to the hopeful comeback of gray whales in the eastern Pacific.

Photographs of the ocean shore show birds and animals that live either in the waters or near the shoreline, including sandpipers, loons, gulls, cormorants, seals, otters, and many sea creatures.

A discussion of puffins, whales, and seals is central to this book. It provides a short list of possible activities that an interested student or class might want to consider undertaking.

## Possible Topics for Further Student Investigation

**1** The puffins shown in this book were photographed along the coast of Alaska and on the Pribilof Islands. Research the birds of Alaska. They are numerous and varied. Then use a detailed map of Alaska to share with your class where various birds make their homes in this vast state. If someone you know has visited Alaska, invite him or her to speak to your class and share slides of birds and other wildlife of Alaska.

**2** In almost every state you will find "adopt a highway" signs indicating that some service club, scouting group, individual family, or other group has agreed to keep a stretch of roadway clear of trash. If you live close to an ocean, stream, or lake, look into having your class or some club or group within the school adopt a section of the shoreline. Try to keep it looking natural and clean. Or, for a short-term project, organize a special cleanup day for your class. Remove the trash that makes shoreline areas unattractive and also poses a variety of hazards to wildlife.

**3** Puffins are particularly colorful and unusual-looking birds. Study the photographs in this book and in other bird books and nature magazines. If you like to draw and sketch wildlife, make some full-color drawings of puffins or other sea birds to share with your classmates. You might want to point out the differences in beaks, bills, legs, and feet that represent adaptations of different birds to their habitat.

---

# 📖 *Wonders of Sharks*

by Wyatt Blassingame
New York: Dodd, Mead, 1984. 96p.

This book contains sixteen short chapters and is illustrated by a number of black-and-white photographs. The book discusses many aspects of sharks, including their physical appearance, evolution, food, senses, reproduction, attacks on humans, and the legends surrounding them. There are sections on sport fishing and on the ways in which sharks have been studied for a variety of research projects.

Wyatt Blassingame is a well-known author who has written hundreds of stories and articles as well as four adult novels and more than fifty books for young readers. Titles of some of his wildlife books are *Wonders of Egrets, Bitterns, and Herons; Skunks; Porcupines;* and *The Strange Armadillo.*

Blassingame begins this book by discussing the fear that people have of sharks. Part of this fear, he believes, is due to misinformation. In the next section of the book, he gives accurate information about the shark's evolution, its body, and its teeth, food, and reproduction.

There is a discussion as to why sharks attack human beings and what sometimes keeps them from attacking. Although many species of sharks do not attack humans, several do. There is detailed information about the man-eaters and about what to do if you should see a shark approaching you in the water.

## Possible Topics for Further Student Investigation

1. The author points out that, per year, three times as many people are killed in the United States by bee stings than are killed throughout the world by sharks. Have you ever wondered what are the major causes of death in people under the age of twenty-one? Research the major causes of death, and some of the extremely rare causes of death, for young people. Prepare this information in a series of graphs. Post the graphs in your room and share them with your class.

2. Cancer, which is fairly common in humans and in most animals, is rare in sharks. Scientists have studied this phenomenon to try to find out why. Some of this research has been carried out at the Mote Marine Laboratory in Sarasota, Florida. Do some research of your own to find out if any information gathered from the study of sharks has been used to try to improve the health of humans. Share what you learn with your classmates.

3. There are many legends and stories about sharks, some of which are discussed in chapter 12 of *Wonders of Sharks.* Write your own shark legend or create a short story in which a shark plays an important role. Have interested friends critique the first draft of your writing. When you have a final, polished draft, share your legend or short story with your class. Include an illustration if you wish.

# Part III
# Understanding, Exploring, and Surviving

# Understanding, Exploring, and Surviving

## ◆ Literature Books ◆

📖*Haunted Journey*
Obie and Blas explore the Tennessee wilderness and make some surprising discoveries

📖*The River*
Brian's adventures in the Canadian wilderness

📖*Seaward*
Strange kingdoms are encountered on Westerly and Cally's journey to the sea

📖*You Must Kiss a Whale*
A desert storm and a whale cause problems for 13-year-old Evelyn and her baby brother Zack

## ◆ Bridge ◆

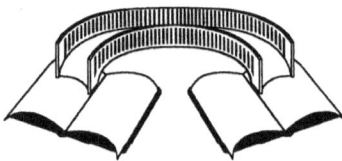

📖*Window on the Deep, the Adventures of Underwater Explorer Sylvia Earle*
Sylvia's adventures at the bottom of the ocean

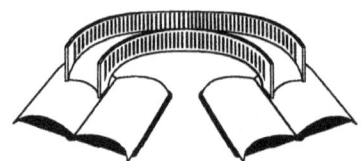

## ◆ Nonfiction Connections ◆

📖*Land Under the Sea*
Oceanographers and oceanography, in words and pictures

📖*River in the Ocean: The Story of the Gulf Stream*
The Atlantic Ocean "river" that has made such a difference in U.S. history

📖*Under the High Seas: New Frontiers in Oceanography*
A narrative history

📖*Water World*
A history of the oceans and their influence on the human world

📖*Waves, Tides and Currents*
Waves are not just for surfing

### OTHER TOPICS TO EXPLORE

| | | |
|---|---|---|
| —Typhoons | —Tsunami | —Deep-sea diving |
| —Captain Cook | —The Norse people | —Water pressure |
| —Jacques Cousteau | —The Congo River | —Scuba diving |
| —John Powell | —The Amazon River | —Captain Bly |
| —High and low tides | —Reefs | —Rip tides |
| —Jules Verne | —Kon-Tiki | |

# 📖 *Literature Books* 📖

## Understanding, Exploring, and Surviving

### ◆ Literature Books ◆

📖*Haunted Journey*
Obie and Blas explore the Tennessee wilderness and make some surprising discoveries

📖*The River*
Brian's adventures in the Canadian wilderness

📖*Seaward*
Strange kingdoms are encountered on Westerly and Cally's journey to the sea

📖*You Must Kiss a Whale*
A desert storm and a whale cause problems for 13-year-old Evelyn and her baby brother Zack

### ◆ Bridge ◆

📖*Window on the Deep, the Adventures of Underwater Explorer Sylvia Earle*
Sylvia's adventures at the bottom of the ocean

### ◆ Nonfiction Connections ◆

📖*Land Under the Sea*
Oceanographers and oceanography, in words and pictures

📖*River in the Ocean: The Story of the Gulf Stream*
The Atlantic Ocean "river" that has made such a difference in U.S. history

📖*Under the High Seas: New Frontiers in Oceanography*
A narrative history

📖*Water World*
A history of the oceans and their influence on the human world

📖*Waves, Tides and Currents*
Waves are not just for surfing

#### OTHER TOPICS TO EXPLORE

—Typhoons
—Captain Cook
—Jacques Cousteau
—John Powell
—High and low tides
—Jules Verne

—Tsunami
—The Norse people
—The Congo River
—The Amazon River
—Reefs
—Kon-Tiki

—Deep-sea diving
—Water pressure
—Scuba diving
—Captain Bly
—Rip tides

# Haunted Journey

by Ruth Riddell

New York: Atheneum, 1988. 215p.

**Type of Book:**
This is a realistic book, with supernatural overtones, that is set in 1931. Using the folksy language of hill people, the story is told in the third person, with a boy, Obie Wilks, as the viewpoint character.

**Setting:**
Tennessee.

**Major Characters:**
Obie Wilks; his friend, Bas Alardice; and Obie's dog, Chaser. These three set out into the wilderness to find the truth about an old legend. During the short portion of the story told at home, Obie's brothers and sisters, a powerful mother, and a teacher named Mrs. Middleton are prominent.

**Other Books by the Author:**
*Ice Warrior* (New York: Atheneum, 1992) and *Shadow Witch* (New York: Atheneum, 1989).

## —PLOT SUMMARY—

Obie Wilks and Bas Alardice, accompanied by Obie's dog, Chaser, set out on foot to explore the Tennessee wilderness beyond the juncture of two rivers. They have heard legends about the Nun Yuna Wis, the protective spirits of the ancient Cherokees, who watch over this ancient burial ground.

Obie's grandfather, Micager Wilks, told about finding pearls in mussels where the two rivers meet and drew a map to show the location. Obie's father, Dalton Wilks, who passed on the legend of the pearls, was known as a great storyteller. As a result, people were unsure about the accuracy of the tales he told about his father's explorations.

When Obie's father dies, Obie decides to follow his grandfather's map to find the river pearls. He hopes to sell these to get the money to pay his father's debts and to be able to save Wilks Hollow, the family home.

Obie knows that if he fails, he and his family will be stuck with being tenant farmers. If he succeeds, Obie hopes that he can leave and perhaps join his Uncle Tully in Michigan and work in an automobile factory.

Obie and Bas take supplies and the dog, Chaser, and set out. Obie's mother does not know that Bas Alardice is with Obie. She does not like the Alardice family and has refused to let her children be friends with any of the Alardices.

It takes longer than Obie and Bas planned to reach the area where the two rivers meet. The map is none too detailed, so they aren't sure if they're in the right place or not. But they finally reach a spot on the Yuda River where Obie finds three small pearls and begins to hope that their trip may be successful after all. Obie plans to explore further in the morning, and Bas intends to hunt for some meat to eat.

That night, the boys sleep in a cave. Obie has a strange dream about a row of people who walk by and stare at him. One holds out a cup of pearls, but Obie can't reach it. The dream makes a strange impression on him.

Obie sets out with Chaser the next day and travels to a spot where he leaves the main stream to explore a strange valley and river. The valley has an eerie air about it. Obie sees the remains of a rock fireplace and four walls of a cabin. In the stream nearby, he pulls in huge mussels. Before long, he has twenty-five good-sized pearls.

Realizing that nightfall is not far off, Obie leaves the valley and sets off for the cave and Bas. For the second time that day, he thinks he smells smoke. Before he gets back to the cave, it is dark. In places, the underbrush is so thick he must crawl through, following Chaser.

When Obie reaches the cave, he finds an angry Bas. Clearly, something is wrong, and Obie tries to find out what it is. Bas admits that he's worried and has been feeling uneasy all day. He too has smelled smoke and has seen fresh tracks from a moccasin and a bear. Bas says he also heard moans and shrieks from an old cabin. Bas is roasting a bobcat for Chaser as it isn't fit meat for humans. Obie eats some anyway.

In order to get Bas to continue with their search, Obie earlier had lied to him about the value of each river pearl. So with Obie's recent find, Bas now believes that they have enough money and wants to go home in the morning.

That night Obie has another dream. A strange old man appears with a crooked stick. He threatens Obie with a knife. Then a fierce wind tears off Obie's hair. Bas awakens him from the nightmare, convinced that the nightmare is the result of the bobcat Obie ate earlier.

The next morning, Obie confesses to Bas that he lied about the value of the pearls. Obie explains that he originally lied to convince his greedy brother, Virgil, to join him. Obie needed Virgil's help because he didn't have a gun and couldn't shoot well. He'd taken all the food his mother could spare, and Obie really needed Bas to stay with him and hunt.

Bas explains that he came out of friendship and not because of the money and for his half of the pearls. That day, Bas keeps Chaser with him to help hunt, and Obie sets off alone. He goes to a different spot and throws his grappling line into the river several times without finding any pearl-bearing mussels.

While he is fishing, Obie feels that someone is watching him. At one point he is frightened by a white-tailed deer. Gradually, one by one, he adds to his collection of pearls. Obie reflects on why it is that he is so small and puny while his younger brother, Virgil, is so much bigger. Yet the responsibility for saving the family, Obie feels, falls on the oldest, not the biggest.

Obie's rope drifts out into the creek, and Obie takes off his shoes and coat and swims after it. He almost gets caught in a sucking hole where he would have drowned. When Obie returns to the spot where he had cooked mussels earlier, he finds that someone or something has come and eaten them.

Obie realizes that he lost in the river the two quarters he'd kept carefully secure in his pocket. This means he won't be able to pay someone on the way home to take them across the river.

Obie hears a strange moaning sound. He rushes back to the cave but does not tell Bas that they now have forty-one pearls. He says he only found three, because he fears that if he tells the truth, Bas will immediately head for home. Obie says they can't go home until they have sixty pearls, enough to allow Obie to pay his debts and still have something in his pockets when he heads north. He asks for Bas's help in building a scow.

Even though he's lost his ferry money, Obie figures they can trade a pearl for the ride across the river so they can make it home on time to pay the note due on his mother's property. Obie knows that even if he succeeds in saving their property, his mother, Mattie Mae, won't like his plans to leave for Michigan. He reflects that although his father wore the pants in the family, his mother was the suspenders.

Obie's attempt to build a scow only gives him another dunking in the river. Bas insists that they go home the next day. If Obie wants more pearls, he knows he'll have to return to the valley, which frightens him. They return to the strange valley, and while Bas hunts, Obie begins fishing.

Obie comes upon a burial mound and, beyond it, in the river, finds a number of large pink pearls. Obie continues to think he hears strange sounds. Again, he falls into the river. He thinks he has drowned this time and meets strange people in his semiconscious state. When he comes to, Obie is with Bas, who explains that he saw Obie shooting down the rapids of the river. Eventually the boys get back to the cave.

Although Obie is weak from his crashing about in the river, they head for home. Obie feels he is being followed by the Nun Yuna Wis. They set out for the Sallapoosa River in a threatening storm and have to use pitch and burn their clothes to make torches to safely cross the river.

In the storm, they continue on until they find a small cave on a ledge. Obie falls asleep and has another strange dream, this time about a pair of dancing white shoes.

The next morning, they head north. Near Bub Torrey's cabin, Bas fires his gun and Torrey comes to take them across the river. He feeds them, gets them warm, and lets them spend the night in his cabin. The boys offer to pay for their keep with a pearl, but Torrey won't take one.

At a store in Ivorsol, they trade a pearl for food and drink. Then they hitch a ride with a logger to Tarnight Mill. Finally, a truck takes them to Graysonia Junction.

At home, Obie invites Bas to spend the night, but his mother won't stand for it and Bas leaves. The next morning, Obie gets up and does his chores. Then he wakes his eight siblings. Obie plans to pay his father's debt with eleven pearls, take twelve pearls with him, and leave ten for his mother. He believes he'll get $17 to $20 per pearl, enough for a new start up north.

But when Obie and his mother get to town and unwrap the pearls, they find only twenty instead of thirty-three. Obie thinks his mother has hidden the other thirteen somewhere. His mother pays her debt with eleven pearls and sells the other nine. When they get home, Obie learns that Virgil has left for California. Little Josh, Obie's brother, says that Virgil paid for his way by giving the truck driver one of the missing pearls.

Mrs. Middleton, a teacher, first sends some books, then a note, and finally comes to see Obie. She knows about his journey and how Virgil stole some of his pearls. Mrs. Middleton tells Obie that auto plants have closed up north and people are out of work and in bread lines. She suggests that if he really wants to escape from the farm, Obie should return to school, get a scholarship, and go to college.

Knowing that Obie will have difficulty with his mother agreeing to let him go on to school, his teacher says that "when reasoning fails, you simply resort to telling." Obie gathers his courage and stands up to his mother. He also defies her by going off to visit Bas. The story ends with Obie hopeful that the future may hold good things after all.

# 📖 Discussion Starters 📖

*Haunted Journey*
by Ruth Riddell

**1** In this book you learn that the Nun Yuna Wis are the protective spirits of the ancient Cherokees. The boys hear strange sounds and have unusual dreams and adventures. Are these supernatural phenomena, related to the spirits, or simply ordinary events to which the boys attach unusual importance? What evidence from the book supports your opinion?

**2** Discuss what you think is the significance of Obie's first dream, in which a row of people walk by him and one holds out to him a cup of pearls that he cannot reach.

**3** Discuss the significance of Obie's second dream, in which a strange old man with a crooked stick threatens Obie with a knife and then a wind comes up and tears off Obie's hair. What role does this dream play in the story?

**4** Discuss the significance of Obie's third dream, in which there are dancing white shoes. What could this possibly mean?

**5** Obie doesn't always tell Bas the whole truth. He withholds information because he believes that if he tells all the truth, Bas will head for home too soon. Do you think Obie should tell the truth or not? If Bas knew the whole truth, would he have left Obie alone to continue to find more pearls? What makes you think this?

**6** Mattie Mae, Obie's mother, is a very strong figure. Does Mattie Mae remind you of other strong mother figures you have read about? In what ways are they similar to or different from Mattie Mae?

**7** One of Obie's dreams for his life is to go to live with Uncle Tully in Michigan. By the end of the story, he has a new dream, to escape the farm by getting a college education. Do you think Obie will escape from the farm? Why or why not?

**8** Mattie Mae continued to hold ill feelings toward the Alardice family. But at the end of the book, Obie is going to break with family tradition and visit his friend Bas. What is the significance of Obie's actions?

**9** A map, drawn by Micager Wilks, plays an important part in this story. Have you read other books in which a map is significant? Discuss the role of the map to this story.

**10** Mrs. Middleton is an influential teacher. She encourages Obie to stand up to his mother. Some people might say she interfered in Obie's life. Criticize or defend the actions of Mrs. Middleton.

# 📖 **Multidisciplinary Activities** 📖

*Haunted Journey*
by Ruth Riddell

**1** Obie wants to join his Uncle Tully in Michigan and escape from the farm by working in an automobile factory. But at just this time in the story, the United States is caught up in the Great Depression. Research this topic. What caused the Great Depression? How did it affect people in different parts of the country? What brought the United States out of its depression? Share what you learn with your class.

**2** Find a large map of Tennessee. Locate a spot where there is a juncture of two rivers. Using this information, prepare a map that might be like the one left by Micager Wilks. Show the Yuda River, Tarnight Mill, Graysonia Junction, Wilks Hollow, Ivorsol, and the Sallapoosa River on your map. Make it to scale and include a legend showing the scale in miles per inch.

**3** In this story there are valuable river pearls. What is the difference, if any, between river and ocean pearls? Do pearls naturally occur in different colors? Are most pearls used in jewelry today natural or cultured or manufactured? What are the most expensive pearls? Share what you learn with your classmates.

# The River

by Gary Paulsen
New York: Delacorte Press, 1991. 132p.

**Type of Book:**

This is a modern-day survival/adventure story told from the viewpoint of a fifteen-year-old boy.

**Setting:**

The first part of the story takes place in northern New York; the majority of the action takes place in the Canadian wilderness.

**Major Characters:**

Fifteen-year-old Brian Robeson; his mother; and Derek Holtzer, a psychologist at a government survival school.

**Other Books by the Author:**

*Dogsong* (New York: Bradbury Press, 1985), *Hatchet* (New York: Bradbury Press, 1987), and *The Winter Room* (New York: Orchard Books, 1989). (*The River* is a sequel to *Hatchet*.)

## —PLOT SUMMARY—

The story opens with three men coming to see Brian Robeson at his home. At first Brian thinks they are from the press because he has been hounded by them since he returned home after surviving alone for fifty-four days after a plane crash in the Canadian woods. But the men aren't reporters. Two are instructors, and one is a psychologist at a government survival school.

Brian learns that they want him to repeat his wilderness experience. At first he is not interested, but he does agree to allow the men to come back later that evening and talk with him and his mother. Brian reflects on the past year, how he has changed since his experience in the woods, which he calls "The Time," and how the divorce of his parents still bothers him. He also thinks about a girl he has met, Deborah, with whom he sometimes discusses The Time.

When he first came back to civilization, Brian went to a counselor. But the counselor couldn't seem to understand Brian's experience. He couldn't understand the thrill Brian had of having newly discovered fire. Brian realizes that the experience changed him. One of the things that is different is that he now has an intense interest in cooking and in food.

That night after dinner, one of the men, Derek Holtzer, returns. Brian's mother thinks Derek is crazy to ask Brian to go back into the Canadian wilderness. But, almost surprising himself, Brian speaks up and says he has to go because he learned something about living there that he could share and that perhaps could help others. Brian's mother says she'll call his father and see if he will permit it.

Two weeks later, after having made detailed plans, Brian sets out in a small plane with Derek. For a moment during the plane ride, Brian panics, remembering the earlier crash that left him alone with a dead pilot at a remote lake. Then he calms himself. He also remembers how strange it felt when he got home, how he had to "rectify" and get used to city life again.

This plane is equipped with all sorts of emergency food and gear, but Brian insists that it all go back with the pilot in the plane or he will not stay. Brian explains to Derek that with all those emergency supplies, what they would be doing would just be a game, not real survival. Derek reluctantly agrees and keeps only an emergency radio and material to take notes.

As soon as the plane leaves, Brian quickly sets to work, feeling somewhat strange in this situation where he is the wiser and more experienced of the two. He knows it will rain soon. They need shelter and a fire. They build a shelter, which Brian knows will leak. He cannot find a fire stone, so he can't build a fire, and there will be no smoke to keep the mosquitoes away.

That night the mosquitoes come and are as bad as Brian remembers. Then it begins to rain, and their shelter proves to be worthless. They take refuge beneath a tree, but it is not much better there during the downpour. The next morning they hunt for food and find a few berries.

As they walk along a cliff near the lake, looking for food, the bank gives way and Brian slides down. He is not hurt, but on the ground, he notices flint rocks that will help them make fire. Their next piece of good luck is finding enough hazelnuts to eat and take the edge off their hunger.

They find a spot for their camp in a depression made when a large tree fell and pulled up roots with it, leaving a hole beneath a shelf of rocks. There is a spring nearby. Derek watches and makes notes while Brian carefully goes about preparing everything he needs to make a fire.

In just a couple of days, Brian begins to feel like he's on a camping trip. They have created a pretty nice camp with pine boughs for beds. They have enough wood for a month. They have hazelnuts, berries, wild plums, clams, and fish in their trap. Brian tells Derek that, unlike his previous wilderness adventure, this experience lacks tension, and that he doesn't think one can really be taught how to survive in the wilderness anyway.

As if in answer to Brain's expressed need for tension, a tremendous storm hits.

The thunder is loud and all around them. Lightning strikes, and Derek reaches out for his radio just before he is hit. Brian is also struck and falls unconscious. When Brian wakes, he can smell something awful like burned hair.

At first Brian thinks that Derek is dead. He remembers how it was when the pilot had the heart attack and died. Brian had felt the pilot's cold skin. Brian touches Derek and finds that he is warm and notices that he is breathing shallowly. Brian tries to use the radio to call for help, but it too has been struck by the lightning and does not work.

Brian hopes that Derek may just be knocked out, as his heart is beating and he is breathing. Brian decides to make Derek comfortable in the hope that he will soon regain consciousness, but even as he thinks this, Brian suspects that Derek's injuries are more serious.

Derek does not come out of the coma, and because he had radioed in the afternoon before to report that all was well, Brian realizes that no one will worry or start looking for them for a week or ten days. Brian tries to remember what he might know about treating a comatose person.

Brian realizes that Derek could go for a week without food, but that he must have water. Brian tries to spoon some water into Derek's mouth, but Derek immediately chokes on it.

Feeling helpless, Brian goes through Derek's briefcase. He finds a map, and as Brian looks at it, he realizes that flowing from the lake is the Necktie River, which runs south about 100 miles to Brannock's Trading Post. Although it would be dangerous, Brian feels he has no choice but to try to get Derek to the trading post.

Brian comes upon a grove of poplars that have been cut and trimmed by beavers. He uses these to fashion a raft, using the trail that the beavers had made to the water to drag down eight logs, each about eight feet long. Brian ties the logs together by using small branches and strips of his clothing.

Before leaving, Brian checks Derek carefully to see if there is any change in his condition. He tries shouting at Derek and sticking him with the knife to see if he registers pain. He does not. Brian concludes that, risky as it is, floating down the river on the raft is Derek's only chance of survival.

Brian puts the briefcase on the raft, takes two spears he has made, a pole and a paddle, and food. After much hard work, Brian gets Derek onto the raft and ties him in place with strips of clothing. Brian leaves a note in their camp in case someone comes looking for them.

As they work their way down the river, Brian gradually learns how to use a pole and the crude paddle he has shaped to keep them from constantly jamming into the banks at curves in the river.

That night, Brian is so tired from lack of sleep and his hard work on the raft that he dozes off. When he wakes, he finds that the river has led them into a lake. He shakes himself wider awake and begins paddling. But as he paddles, he half dreams and half hallucinates. He even finds himself thinking how much better it would be if he cut Derek loose and there was only one man left on the raft.

Brian begins to question the wisdom of trusting the map. The one lake he's found did not show up on the map. Was it just a low area, filled with water, and not a permanent lake? Or is the map faulty, and if so, will there be a trading post where it is indicated on the map?

Worried about Derek, Brian pauses long enough to fashion a sort of canopy to protect Derek from the sun. Then he pushes ahead on the river. When the river narrows, as indicated on the map, Brian believes in the map again. Then he hears a strange sound and realizes they are heading toward a waterfall or chute. There is no way to reach shore in time, so they go down the rapids. They hit a rock, and Brian falls off the raft. He sees the raft continue down the river with Derek on it.

Then Brian is slammed down in the water, hits his head, and loses consciousness. When he wakes, he is in the shallow water below the rapids, and the raft is nowhere in sight. Brian tries to run along the bank but finally realizes that if he is to catch the raft, he must swim. Tired as he is, Brian begins to swim down the river.

Finally, Brian catches up with the raft and finds Derek on it, still alive. Almost as if in a dream, Brian continues to paddle down the river, hour after hour. He loses track of time but finally hears a dog bark and sees the roof of a house and a dock. Brian calls out for help to a boy on the shore before he collapses.

The final chapter relates information about how far Brian and Derek traveled on the raft and how long it took. It also explains that Derek recovered completely and that Brian suffered few ill effects from his experiences, although his parents swore never to let him go into the woods again. The book concludes with the arrival of a gift for Brian some months later. It is a sixteen-foot canoe from Derek. Lettered in gold on each side of the bow is "The Raft."

## 📖 Discussion Starters 📖

### *The River*
### by Gary Paulsen

**1** When the three men arrive at Brian's door and suggest that Brian go back into the wilderness, Brian at first thinks the idea is crazy. By that evening, however, Brian is eager to go. What do you think causes him to change his mind?

**2** Bill Mannerly and Erik Ballard are introduced to the reader in chapter one. These characters don't speak, and they never appear again. Why do you think they are included in the story at all? What is their function?

**3** Brian realizes that the relationship between him and his mother is significantly different from what it was before his wilderness experience. Discuss in what ways the relationship has changed and what you think are the reasons for the change.

**4** Brian's mother and father are recently divorced. His mother is seeing another man, and his father is planning to marry another woman. These relationships are not an important part of the story. Why do you suppose the author chose to have Brian's parents be divorced? How would the story be different if they were still a happily married couple?

**5** When it comes time to choose who will stay with Brian, a man who is a trained survivalist or one who is trained to observe and take notes, the observer is selected. If you were in charge, would you make the same decision? Why or why not?

**6** Brian points out that food is very important to him. Find some passages in the book where there are comments about food. What makes these sections so effective?

**7** Deborah McKenzie plays a very small role in this novel. Why do you think this character is included in the story?

**8** In the book, you learn that Brian had a hatchet with him on his first wilderness adventure. On his second adventure, he has a knife with him. He also finds a map. If you were going to be dropped into the wilderness to survive on your own, what one thing would you choose to have with you, and why?

**9** In the final chapter, "Measurements," it is stated that Derek would probably have recovered from his injury even if Brian had not made the run down the river. If you were in Brian's situation, would you wait at the campsite, or would you go down the river? Why?

**10** There is a moment in the story when Brian reflects that everything would be easier if Derek would simply slip off the raft so that Brian would no longer have to be responsible for him. Later, Brian is ashamed to have had this thought. Was it normal for Brian to have had such a thought? Have you ever felt "stuck" with a responsibility you didn't want? How did you handle it?

# 📖 **Multidisciplinary Activities** 📖

*The River*
by Gary Paulsen

**1** Derek taught Brian how to use a hand-held radio. If this radio had not been destroyed by lightning, Brian could simply have called for help. Perhaps you are interested in becoming an amateur ("ham") radio operator. You can be licensed at any age. To earn a license, you will need to take written tests and, possibly, Morse code tests. There are sure to be radio amateurs in your area, and there may even be an amateur radio club. Try to make connections with a local group of "hams." Write to: Educational Activities Department, Amateur Radio Relay League, 225 Main Street, Newington, CT 06111-1494 and request general information on amateur radio, licensing requirements, recommended study materials, and clubs in your area.

**2** Obtain a topographical map for a section of a park or wilderness area near you. Learn how to read the contour lines on the map. Plan several hikes into the area. Mark your hikes on the map and indicate the amount of elevation change from one spot to another. Rate your hikes as easy, medium, or hard, taking into account not only distances involved but elevation loss or gain. Estimate how long each round-trip hike would take. Have a knowledgeable person check your final work to see how you did in your map reading and trip planning.

**3** Brian searches hard to find a fire stone to start his fire. You can also make a fire by friction and by focusing sunlight through a lens onto tinder. With a scout leader or experienced outdoors person, practice different ways of making an outdoor fire. Be sure to have supervision and to take fire safety precautions. Carefully write up each step in your fire-starting process (just as Brian does) and share your detailed explanation with the class.

# 📖 *Seaward*

by Susan Cooper
New York: Margaret K. McElderry, 1983. 167p.

### Type of Book:
This is a fantasy told from the viewpoints of the two major characters, a boy and a girl, both about age sixteen, named Westerly and Cally.

### Setting:
Strange kingdoms that lie on the route the teenagers are taking toward the sea.

### Major Characters:
Westerly and Cally, two teenagers journeying to the sea; Lugan and Lady Taranis, who represent Life and Death; a stonecutter; Ryan, who lives in the stonecutter's cottage; and Peth, a mosquito-like creature.

### Other Books by the Author:
*The Dark Is Rising* (New York: Atheneum, 1973), *Greenwitch* (New York: Atheneum, 1974), and *The Grey King* (New York: Atheneum, 1975).

## —PLOT SUMMARY—

As the story opens, Westerly has been walking for half a day. He's thirsty, hungry, and feels that he is being followed. He stops at a stream to drink some water and catch a fish. He performs a ceremony with bones and is warned of danger.

Next, Cally's story begins. She's been climbing in the apple tree and has scratched her hand. Cally has strange hands with rough, thick skin at the base of each finger. She is worried about her sick father, who she sees being taken to a hospital by the sea in a car with a white-haired woman dressed in blue.

Although busy in school, Cally notices that her mother looks ill. Mother finally asks if Cally would mind being left at home with Aunt Tess until school is out so that she can leave immediately to visit Cally's father and have some medical tests done. Cally agrees. That night she hears her mother humming a strange tune.

The next day, the car comes again with the same white-haired woman; this time it is Cally's mother who is driven away. Aunt Tess won't arrive for two days, so Cally is on her own until then. She makes a cup of tea and then hears the strange melody that she had heard her mother humming. It seems to come from nowhere. The next morning, Cally hears the tune again. She calls her friend, Jen.

Jen suggests it may just be the wind. But the tune comes again, like a call to the sea. Cally stands in front of her mother's mirror. She presses her hand against the glass and steps through the mirror and into a strange land.

Westerly, still on his journey, hears distant voices, the clash of metal, and the sound of horses. Suddenly he looks over a plateau and sees clusters of men in blue or gold. He has stumbled upon a game of chess being played on the field by blue- and gold-robed men. He sees a gold-robed man and a blue-robed woman on a hill. The blue-robed woman says that Westerly should not be there. Westerly explains that he came through a door, which he entered by following the directions of his mother. The blue-robed woman says Westerly will be caught if he tries to run away across the plains.

Westerly decides to take his chances among the gold-clad chessmen. For a time, he follows orders and stands where told, but finally he breaks out of the game and runs for his life. As he does so, all the knights on the field disappear.

When Westerly reaches the edge of the trees, he sees a log house. The gold-robed man from the top of the hill invites him in. Westerly hesitates. He is on his way to the sea to find his father, and his mother told him that he would meet only three beings that he could trust on the way: a man with owl eyes, a girl with selkie hands, and a creature in a "high place." Westerly decides to trust this man because he has owl-like eyes. The man says his name is Lugan, that he knew Westerly's mother, and that he is Westerly's watchman and sees all that happens to him.

Lugan explains that the woman in blue is Lady Taranis. For protection, Lugan gives Westerly a box and a small bundle wrapped in red cloth. Music fills the cabin, and Lady Taranis turns the cabin into a forest and tries to captivate Westerly.

But Lugan populates the forest with dragons from his box and sends Westerly on his way alone. Before long, Westerly finds a small boat and begins to row on a river.

Cally has stepped through the mirror and into a wood. She walks along a path until she comes to a giant pillar. On the top of the pillar are two faces, one gentle and the other fierce. Cally briefly sees a woman in a blue cloak who disappears. Giant stone figures arise from the boulders and begin to chase Cally.

Cally runs to a stonecutter, who explains that these are "The People," stone creatures by night, awakened by the sun during the day. Cally goes into the stonecutter's house and meets Ryan, a gray-haired woman who is cleaning the floor. Ryan sends her out to get sand and dock.

Ryan uses the dock to put a special stain on the floor and uses the sand to mark the hearth. She explains that this will protect the house for a month, and she advises Cally not to remain long, or the stonecutter will keep her for Lady Taranis.

Lady Taranis suddenly appears in the cottage and is challenged by Ryan. Lady Taranis tries to coax Cally out, but Ryan's magic keeps her away. Lady Taranis leaves but says she'll be back.

That night, Cally discovers that the stonecutter also turns to stone at night because he is under Lady Taranis's spell. Ryan explains that the stonecutter has something of hers and so she must stay. She gives Cally a message to deliver and sends Cally on her way to the sea.

Ryan tells Cally that if she needs help, she should call on the birds of Rhiannon of the Roane. Cally leaves, following a stream toward the sea. She sees Westerly in his boat. He takes her across the water to a castle that they see.

Inside are many rooms. Above one door is Cally's name—"Calliope." It leads to a bedroom that Cally has often dreamed of. They find another door marked "Westerly." Westerly enters it, but Cally cannot. It, too, is a room in a dream world.

From their windows, they see The People coming. Westerly is able to bring Cally with him into his dream room, where there is a trapdoor that leads to the roof. The stonecutter pursues them. Cally calls for the birds of Rhiannon of the Roane. Westerly pulls out a little dragon from his box, which grows huge. The stonecutter turns the dragon to stone.

Westerly uses his knife against the stonecutter without success, but the stonecutter is killed when he falls against the dragon. Before he dies, he turns Cally into stone. Lady Taranis comes and makes an offer to Westerly, which he refuses. She leaves. Then the birds come, and each drops a feather on the stone figure of Cally. Magically, she comes back to life, and Cally and Westerly go back into the castle.

They go underground. While they are there, the castle collapses above them. A huge snake appears in the cavern and whisks them away into the dark. The snake says he is "Time Present and Time Future" saving them from the "Past."

Then Cally finds herself swimming like a selkie, a seal who is human when it puts aside its skin. The snake explains that those of selkie blood always dream of the sea. If a selkie puts aside her skin to swim as a girl, and a man finds her, she must stay with him as long as her skin is hidden. The snake also reveals to Cally that her parents are dead.

Cally and Westerly are then released and find themselves back in the boat. Cally seems so happy after her adventures with the snake that Westerly is jealous. He jumps out of the boat and leaves Cally to float away while he walks to shore, where he meets Lugan.

Lugan and Westerly run to help Cally and her boat through the locks. They see another cottage, out of which Lady Taranis steps. She demands a toll or a life. Lugan tells Westerly to use the bundle he gave him. Westerly and Cally run, and a giant wave suddenly comes and envelopes Lugan. Westerly tears open the bundle, and a huge wind carries him and Cally away.

After a terrible time in the wind, the two find themselves on sand dunes. They walk for hours across the sand toward a mountain. That night, they share the contents of their packs, put up a tent, and sleep. They continue walking for two days; each night, they hear a strange sound as if a bird is calling.

Then a strange creature like a giant insect appears. It says its name is Peth and that it has been looking for them. It urges them to travel quickly in the night. Peth leads them out of the dunes to a flat place. He explains that it used to be a sea until Lady Taranis stole it.

They continue traveling and see puffs of dust. Something is following them. Peth continues to lead the way. Then he builds a sort of spider's web to conceal them. The pursuers come and then disappear. Peth also teaches Westerly more about the three bones he carries and the powers that they have.

Using the magic bones, Westerly makes it rain. He and Cally drink and eat and are revived. After the rain, the Valley of the White Sea blooms. Westerly and Cally eat delicious blossoms. Then Peth leads them up through the mountains.

When they are finally in sight of the last ridge, Peth collapses and dies. From the top of the ridge they see trees before them and, in the distance, the sea. Suddenly the two-faced pillar appears. The friendly face smiles at them, but the fierce face glares. Cally and Westerly seem unable to move forward, and it begins to snow.

Cally and Westerly grope a little farther down the trail and then pitch a tent and wait inside while it continues to blow and snow. Westerly remembers what Peth taught him and uses the magic of the three bones to call out the sun to melt the snow.

Once down from the mountain, they reach a road filled with silent people. Cally and Westerly join the silent crowd and walk toward a gate that leads to the sea. At the gateway, Cally says her name. Bells go off, and Cally and Westerly are locked in a small stone room. Then there is a blurring, and the white walls retreat. They see Lugan and Lady Taranis.

Lugan explains that only the dead can go through the gates and that not all of the dead wish to go to the sea, only those who took and gave pleasure in life. These folk go to the islands of Tir Na n'Og and live forever young without hurt or change. Lugan represents Life and Lady Taranis, his sister, is Death.

Westerly chooses to go to the island to find his father. Cally keeps her promise by giving Ryan's message to the seal. Then Ryan appears and rushes into the sea to take her seal shape again. She calls to Cally to join them, but Cally chooses not to. Then Cally's hands become smooth. Lugan explains that this happened because she chose not to be a selkie.

Suddenly Westerly comes running back up the beach. He announces he will not go without Cally. The two of them decide to return to their own world and live. Lugan says they must go alone and will at first not remember their adventures, but he promises that before long they will meet and begin their lives together.

# 📖 **Discussion Starters** 📖

*Seaward*
by Susan Cooper

**1** This story uses the viewpoints of two different characters, first Westerly and then Cally. It alternates back and forth between the two until the characters finally meet. Was it easy for you to switch back and forth between the two story lines? What do you gain or lose as a storyteller when you use more than one viewpoint character?

**2** Part of the urgency in this story is achieved by the fact that Westerly always feels he is being followed. Yet, exactly what it is that is following him always remains unclear. Find some of these pursuit passages in the book. What makes them so effective in creating tension and mood?

**3** There is a duality in this book. There are two main viewpoint characters, Westerly and Cally. Life and Death are represented by a brother and sister. The giant pillar has two faces. What other dual qualities can you find throughout the book?

**4** Inside the castle, Cally finds her "dream room," and Westerly finds his. Each is different. If you were to find your dream room, what would it look like?

**5** You learn about the strange appearance of Cally's hands early in the story. When you first learned about them, what did you think? Did you think this would be important to the story? Did you guess her unusual ancestry?

**6** One of the most unusual characters in the book is Peth. The People and the disappearing chesspieces are strange but have humanlike forms. Why do you suppose Peth looks like an insect? What does this characteristic add to the story?

**7** The book is filled with magic spells of one kind or another, such as Cally calling on the birds, Westerly making it rain, and Ryan painting symbols on the floor of the cottage. Which of the magic spells in the book was most interesting to you and why?

**8** The People are very strange creatures. They have no eyes and their arms are handless. They are half people-shaped and half stone-shaped. Why do you suppose the author chose to make them so "formless"?

**9** When Cally and Westerly reached the road filled with silent people all walking toward one destination, what did you think was happening? What details made you think that? Did you immediately guess that these people were all dead?

**10** Cally and Westerly are told that, when they go back to their former lives, they will not immediately remember their adventure and they will not be together. But they are promised that, before long, they will meet each other. If you were responsible for creating a situation in which they meet again, what would that situation be?

# 📖 **Multidisciplinary Activities** 📖

*Seaward*
by Susan Cooper

**1** Ryan rejoins the seals at the end of this story. There are several different types of seals, found in different parts of the world. Research seals. How many kinds of seals are there? Where is each type found? Using the information you have gained, make a map of the world and locate various seal populations, showing both the type of seal and where it is commonly located. Share your map with the class.

**2** For seemingly endless days, Cally and Westerly hike across sand dunes. What causes sand dunes? Are there more than one kind? Where are the major sand dunes in the world located? On a map of the world, locate the major sand dune areas. Share this information with your class.

**3** Peth is an imaginary insect, but he is strong, and he can make a web. Spiders make many different kinds of webs, which are easiest to see when they are covered in moisture, such as morning dew. Where might you locate different webs? Find some and photograph them. You may need close-up lenses to get good pictures. After you have photographed several webs, noting the time and place of each picture, do some research and try to find out which type of spider made each of the webs. Share your pictures and identifications with your classmates.

# 📖 *You Must Kiss a Whale*

by David Skinner

New York: Simon and Schuster Books for Young Readers, 1992. 94p.

**Type of Book:**
   Told in the first person, this book has elements of fantasy, science fiction, mystery, and realism.

**Setting:**
   Joan Blos, Newbery Medal-winning author, says that this story is "set in the strange yet familiar landscape of the mind." The actual setting is a desert near the town of Soso, but it includes a core image of a beached whale.

**Major Characters:**
   Thirteen-year-old Evelyn; her mother; and her baby brother, Zack.

**Other Books by the Author:**
   This is the first novel by David Skinner.

## —PLOT SUMMARY—

Thirteen-year-old Evelyn has moved with her mother and her baby brother, Zack, to a strange desert. They live as squatters in an old, abandoned house among juniper trees and tumbleweeds. They have no phone and no mail delivery. The closest town, Soso, is about thirty miles away.

This strange spot was chosen because a predictable and violent storm constantly hits the area. Evelyn's mother spends all of her time tracking and gathering data about "the storm" and working on a secret project in a tent out in the yard. (The reader later learns that the secret project is making the "Ultimate Raincoat.")

Only a year prior to the opening of the story, Evelyn lived in a perfectly ordinary house in an ordinary suburb, had started eighth grade, and had a best friend named Michelle. But all this changed when Evelyn's father left his family. He had disappeared before, but this time it seems he is gone for good. Now, deserted by her father and ignored by her mother, and having moved into a strange new place without friends, Evelyn spends her days preparing food for the family and caring for her brother, Zack, in a dilapidated house where every room is cluttered with debris from constant storm damage.

In one room in the house, far from the kitchen, Evelyn comes upon her mother's old chest, unlocked and filled with all sorts of strange things that she has brought along with her.

Although she feels she should not invade her mother's privacy, Evelyn can't resist looking in the trunk. She takes out one item at a time and, when she is finished, carefully puts it back in its original place so that the trunk contents appear undisturbed.

Among the mementos in the trunk, Evelyn finds a stack of old papers covered in her father's very poor handwriting. Words have been crossed out and scrawls have been added in the margins. It is a messy document, and Evelyn must almost translate, word for word, to understand it.

Evelyn soon learns that the handwritten pages contain a story, which she begins to read. In this way, a "story within a story" is introduced in the book. From the trunk manuscript, the reader learns about eight-year-old Kevin, his mother, and his little brother, Matt.

The manuscript tells how Kevin becomes ill and stays home in bed while his mother takes time off from work to care for him. Kevin is bedeviled by Matt and recovers slowly. While ill, Kevin receives a strange letter, containing a single sentence. The mysterious letter was sent from a coastal town where Kevin knows no one.

The message says, "You must kiss a whale." Or at least that's what Kevin *thinks* it says. The writing is so messy that he can't be absolutely sure. Sometimes Kevin thinks it might say, "You must kill a whale."

When Kevin is finally well, he decides to investigate his strange message by taking a cab to explore the coastal town from which it was sent. On the drive, the talkative cabby learns a good deal about Kevin and his mission.

Kevin gives the cabby the letter to read, and he agrees that the handwriting is so poor it is hard to interpret. The cabby suggests that they stop at the local university campus and visit the office of a linguistics professor to see what she can make of the note.

Kevin goes to an office in Morrill Hall to consult with Cornelia Lopez. Professor Lopez is a busy and impatient woman. One day when she came into her office, she explains to Kevin, she found that all the words had slipped out of the pages of her books, covering the shelves and floors like a slippery ash. She's tried to put the words back, but still has a few left over.

Professor Lopez shows her list of leftover words to Kevin and suggests that her words are much more difficult to make sense of than his.

Professor Lopez looks at Kevin's letter and insists that it says, "You must kirr a whale." Kevin maintains there is no such word as *kirr*, but the professor explains that every word has a birth and that *kirr* is a newborn word.

Unconvinced, Kevin returns to the cab, only to learn that there is now great excitement in town. It seems that a whale has come up on the beach.

Kevin goes to the beach and manages to get close to the whale. It is a scene of great confusion. Souvenir hunters are trying to take bits and pieces of the whale.

Nature lovers are trying to find ways to help the whale survive by putting wet towels on him. City fathers are trying to decide what they should do next.

Kevin meets a vagrant who strikes up a conversation with him in which he tells Kevin that he is omniscient. The vagrant turns out to be the man who wrote the strange letter to Kevin. Standing near the beached whale, Kevin asks, "So should I go kill it?" And Evelyn's father's manuscript simply ends at this point.

In the meantime, a violent desert storm is approaching Evelyn and her family in the old, isolated house. Mother announces that she has finished the Ultimate Raincoat. It is a raincoat "that isn't there" and that the storm "can't touch." At this point, Evelyn fears that her mother has gone completely mad.

When Mother discovers that Evelyn has gone into her private chest, Evelyn explains finding her father's story and reading it and how the story was left unfinished. Mother explains that she knows about the unfinished story.

Mother begins to cry and begs Evelyn not to run away from her. Evelyn is surprised at this reaction because she feels that, in fact, it is Mother who has run away from her.

Evelyn decides to write an ending for her father's story. In her ending, the vagrant insists that the letter does not say that Kevin must *kill* the whale but rather that he must *kiss* the whale. This will give the whale the sort of comfort that all living creatures need. So Kevin kisses the whale, and both he and the whale are happy.

As the storm abates in the desert, Mother suggests that she and Evelyn and Zack pack up and leave in the morning and move to someplace where the weather is normal. They do.

In the epilogue to the book, Zack, who is now in first grade, phones his sister, Evelyn, who is now in college. Mother's voice is heard in the background.

Evelyn has come to some understanding of both her father and her mother. She reflects that you can't always expect perfect endings, and that "every day is the final day for one thing or another, finished or not."

# 📖 Discussion Starters 📖

*You Must Kiss a Whale*
by David Skinner

**1** What is the connection between the main story (Evelyn, Zack, and their mother living out in the desert) and the story Evelyn finds told in a manuscript hidden away in the trunk (involving Kevin, Matt, and their mother)?

**2** What is the significance of the Ultimate Raincoat?

**3** Even though the desert storm almost destroys the house in which Evelyn and her family find shelter, the storm is always predictable, down to the minute. What is the significance to the rest of the story of this predictability?

**4** When Mother turns to Evelyn and begs, "Please don't ever run away from me," Evelyn is both surprised and confused. Evelyn thinks, Just who's run away from whom? In this story, who really is running away? From what is Mother running? From what is Evelyn running? What does each find to help them stop running away?

**5** The abandoned house they live in is like a disaster area. It is filled with broken glass, is water soaked, has smashed walls and roof, and has fallen timbers. For what is this damaged house with its many broken rooms a symbol?

**6** On page 73 of the book, what do you think Mother means when she boldly says, "No more defeats"?

**7** Mother makes things out of mislaid thoughts as well as out of metal and plastic. One thing she has made is a story that she has often told Evelyn about a storm in her hometown that included blind and destructive monsters. What does this anecdote, which Evelyn calls a "lie," have to do with the main story?

**8** Professor Lopez describes coming into her office and finding that all the words have slipped off the pages of her books. She tried to put them back but says that for six months afterwards, she kept finding words in her clothes, hair, and food. What does this strange incident have to do with the main story line?

**9** Other than the family, Evelyn refers to only one other person by name, her old best friend, Michelle. At one point, Evelyn even thinks she sees Michelle in a store in Soso even though, in reality, Michelle is a thousand miles away. What is the importance of Michelle to this story?

**10** In the story within a story, the mother appears to be quite different from Evelyn's mother. How are the two mothers alike and how are they different?

# 📖 **Multidisciplinary Activities** 📖

*You Must Kiss a Whale*
by David Skinner

**1** A beached whale, like the one in this story, is hard to move because of its great size. When we measure things that are especially small or especially large, we use different units of measure. These units of measure have developed over a long period of time. Choose some units of measure that are of interest to you. Trace their history. Explain how they came into common use and how they have been refined. Among these might be *cubit*, *span*, *foot*, *uncia*, *inch*, *reach*, and *fathom*. Share what you learn with your class.

**2** The linguistics professor suggests that the word in the note that Kevin can't read is *kirr*. Kevin says this isn't a word. The professor argues that it is a "newborn" word. Words come into common usage every day. Find a dozen words that have come into common usage since 1900. For each of your dozen words, give its definition and explain how it came into use. Include your words and definitions in a chart to put on the class bulletin board.

**3** Evelyn's mother was trying to invent the Ultimate Raincoat. Backpackers, fishermen, and hikers would also love to have the "ultimate" raincoat when they find themselves caught in a downpour. Companies have tried many different materials to make the ultimate raincoat. Thumb through some current sporting goods catalogues. Are there any coats guaranteed to be waterproof? What are they made of? How is such material manufactured? How does it compare with other materials in terms of cost and comfort? Share what you learn in an oral report to your class.

# 📖 *Bridge* 📖

## Understanding, Exploring, and Surviving

---

### ◆ Literature Books ◆

📖*Haunted Journey*
Obie and Blas explore the Tennessee wilderness and make some surprising discoveries

📖*The River*
Brian's adventures in the Canadian wilderness

📖*Seaward*
Strange kingdoms are encountered on Westerly and Cally's journey to the sea

📖*You Must Kiss a Whale*
A desert storm and a whale cause problems for 13-year-old Evelyn and her baby brother Zack

---

### ◆ Bridge ◆

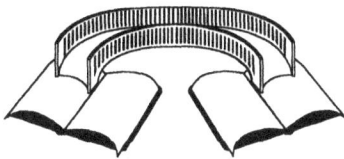

📖*Window on the Deep, the Adventures of Underwater Explorer Sylvia Earle*
Sylvia's adventures at the bottom of the ocean

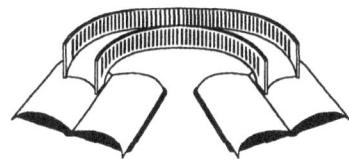

---

### ◆ Nonfiction Connections ◆

📖*Land Under the Sea*
Oceanographers and oceanography, in words and pictures

📖*River in the Ocean: The Story of the Gulf Stream*
The Atlantic Ocean "river" that has made such a difference in U.S. history

📖*Under the High Seas: New Frontiers in Oceanography*
A narrative history

📖*Water World*
A history of the oceans and their influence on the human world

📖*Waves, Tides and Currents*
Waves are not just for surfing

#### OTHER TOPICS TO EXPLORE

—Typhoons
—Captain Cook
—Jacques Cousteau
—John Powell
—High and low tides
—Jules Verne

—Tsunami
—The Norse people
—The Congo River
—The Amazon River
—Reefs
—Kon-Tiki

—Deep-sea diving
—Water pressure
—Scuba diving
—Captain Bly
—Rip tides

# 📖 *Window on the Deep, the Adventures of Underwater Explorer Sylvia Earle*

by Andrea Conley
New York: Franklin Watts, 1991. 44p.

This is a large-format, easy-to-read book with many color photographs. The book is one of a series done in conjunction with the New England Aquarium. This biographical work makes an excellent bridge between fiction and nonfiction.

Chapter one deals with the account of Sylvia Earle, who, in 1979, became the first person to stand, unconnected by surface support, 1,250 feet below the surface of the ocean off the island of Oahu. It describes how she descends, strapped to a platform of a small submarine named *Star II*, and what happens after she frees herself from the platform and begins to look about.

Chapter two tells how Earle led the first all-women's team of aquanauts on a two-week underwater expedition during which they used scuba equipment and lived at a specially equipped underwater hotel.

Chapter three explains how Earle worked with a British technical engineer named Graham Hawkes to build a submersible named *Deep Rover*. This new submersible is lightweight, battery-operated, inexpensive, and has a large transparent sphere for viewing, and arms and suction devices for examining and collecting specimens. It took five years to build *Deep Rover*. Sylvia Earle took *Deep Rover* down to 3,000 feet below the surface.

Later chapters discuss the development of *Deep Flight I* and *Deep Flight II*, underwater gliders that will move at more than thirteen miles per hour and allow for exploration of deep-water trenches.

## Possible Topics for Further Student Investigation

1. Page 13 of *Window on the Deep* has a detailed picture of a Jim Suit. This specially constructed suit was named after the diver Jim Jarratt. The book gives you no other information about Jarratt. Use him as a topic for library research. Where might you find information about him? Using your best investigative skills, learn what you can about Jim Jarratt. Share with the class both the information that you find and a brief explanation of how you went about your research and what specific references you used.

2. The Jim Suit is used to resist water pressure. Find out more about atmospheric pressure and water pressure. Make a chart to show the amount of pressure in pounds over our bodies that we experience on the surface of the earth and at different depths of the water. Sylvia Earle hopes to explore trenches at the bottom of the ocean that are more than 6,000 feet deep. What would be the pressure at that depth?

3. Sylvia Earle is quoted as saying that "there is life in every teaspoon of water." Collect some pond water. Try to collect it from different spots of the pond and at different depths. Label each specimen so that you will know where and when you collected it. Study the pond water that you collect with your naked eye, with a magnifying glass, and with a microscope. Can you find any living creatures? Make sketches of what you see. Try to identify anything that you find. Share what you learn with your classmates.

# 📖 *Nonfiction Connections* 📖

## Understanding, Exploring, and Surviving

---

### ◆ Literature Books ◆

📖*Haunted Journey*
Obie and Blas explore the Tennessee wilderness and make some surprising discoveries

📖*The River*
Brian's adventures in the Canadian wilderness

📖*Seaward*
Strange kingdoms are encountered on Westerly and Cally's journey to the sea

📖*You Must Kiss a Whale*
A desert storm and a whale cause problems for 13-year-old Evelyn and her baby brother Zack

---

### ◆ Bridge ◆

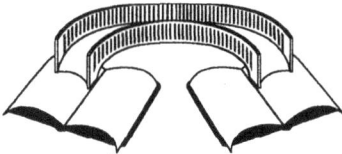

📖*Window on the Deep, the Adventures of Underwater Explorer Sylvia Earle*
Sylvia's adventures at the bottom of the ocean

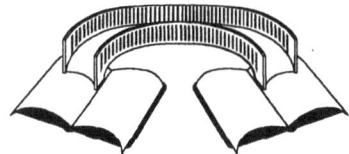

---

### ◆ Nonfiction Connections ◆

📖*Land Under the Sea*
Oceanographers and oceanography, in words and pictures

📖*River in the Ocean: The Story of the Gulf Stream*
The Atlantic Ocean river that has made such a difference in U.S. history

📖*Under the High Seas: New Frontiers in Oceanography*
A narrative history

📖*Water World*
A history of the oceans and their influence on the human world

📖*Waves, Tides and Currents*
Waves are not just for surfing

#### OTHER TOPICS TO EXPLORE

—Typhoons
—Captain Cook
—Jacques Cousteau
—John Powell
—High and low tides
—Jules Verne

—Tsunami
—The Norse people
—The Congo River
—The Amazon River
—Reefs
—Kon-Tiki

—Deep-sea diving
—Water pressure
—Scuba diving
—Captain Bly
—Rip tides

# 📖 *Land Under the Sea*

## by Hershell H. Nixon and Joan Lowery Nixon
New York: Dodd, Mead, 1985. 62p.

This is a short book with easy-to-read text that is illustrated by black-and-white drawings and photographs. It provides a simple and interesting introduction to oceanography.

The book begins with a discussion of some of the early explorers of the land beneath the waters, beginning with Matthew Fontaine Maury, who, in 1855, published his book *The Physical Geography of the Sea*. Other explorers included are the scientists from the British ship *H.M.S. Challenger*; Ewing, Heezen, and Press, scientists from the Woods Hole Oceanographic Institution who worked together in 1947; and Marie Tharp, who gathered information from many ships that sailed the oceans and recorded data using depth finders.

There is a section on the oceanographer's tools including the Scripps Sea Beam System, sonar, and Deep Tow, as well as a discussion of the ocean-drilling programs of *Glomar Challenger*; of *Alvin*, which is carried on a mother ship called *Atlantis II*; and of the French ship *Cyana*.

Another section of the book is devoted to an explanation of the geography of the land beneath the sea, including the continental shelf, the continental slope, ocean trenches, troughs and ridges, ocean basins, midocean canyons, plateaus, seamounts, coral reefs and atolls, the midocean ridge, and undersea volcanoes.

## Possible Topics for Further Student Investigation

**1** This book suggests that charts of the world ocean floor panorama are available in different sizes. The Scripps Institute of Oceanography or the Woods Hole Oceanographic Institution could probably supply you with an address where you could write to secure information on the prices of these various-sized charts, which might be of use to your science class. Investigate the possibility of having your school science department purchase one to share with the class.

**2** Many people do not realize that volcanoes may erupt on the ocean floor much as they erupt on land. Study both kinds of volcanic eruptions. If possible, find pictures of the different kinds of lava flows. Use drawings and charts to explain to your classmates the similarities of and differences between volcanic eruptions on land and on the ocean floor.

**3** Telephone cables have been laid across the ocean floor. This might make an interesting topic for research. When were the first cables laid? What was the initial cost of laying the cables? What is their route in the ocean? What were the major problems in initially laying the cables? What problems have arisen since? Do the cables often break or need repair? How are repairs accomplished? Are these cables still important or have they been totally replaced by communication satellites? Share what you learn.

# 📖 *River in the Ocean: The Story of the Gulf Stream*

by Alice Gilbreath
Minneapolis, Minn.: Dillon Press, 1986. 96p.

This short book, illustrated with color photographs, provides a good introduction to the Gulf Stream.

The book begins with some facts and a map of the Gulf Stream. It explains the circular pattern of the various currents in the northern Atlantic Ocean and suggests that the Gulf Stream's banks can be thought of simply as layers of cold ocean water on both sides of this big river.

Chapter two discusses eddies, whirlpools, the Labrador Current, and the Sargasso Sea. Chapter three explains how early explorers contributed to our knowledge about currents in the ocean. It also describes a question that Benjamin Franklin faced when he was postmaster general: Why did the mail ships from England to New York take longer than the merchant ships that sailed from England to Rhode Island? By talking with ship captains, Franklin found out about the effects of the current and gave it the name Gulf Stream. Franklin also made a fairly accurate chart of the Gulf Stream in 1769.

The book goes on to discuss superstitions of the sea and discoveries made by using submersibles. It also explains what happens when warm and cold currents meet and how weather is affected by oceans, and it explores ways in which the oceans can help to feed the populations of the world.

## Possible Topics for Further Student Investigation

**1** Using an overhead projector, trace a large world map. Label the continents and the various oceans and seas. Using different colored markers, show the Gulf Stream, the Labrador Current, the North Atlantic Current, the Canary Current, and the North Equatorial Current. Show which of these currents are warm and which are cold. Indicate in what directions they flow. Display your project on a class bulletin board.

**2** Chapter eight of this book is devoted to the effect of the oceans and seas on our weather. One dramatic form of weather is the hurricane. Study hurricanes, how they are formed, when they usually occur, and what parts of the United States are most often hit by them. Create some charts and use them to explain to your classmates how hurricanes form. Take at least one hurricane that has been well documented, trace its path, and discuss the destruction that it caused.

**3** This book explains that research is being conducted into how oceans might supply food to feed our world population. Although sea food is available now in all parts of the country (either fresh or flown in to stores), it is not a popular food. Suppose that you are a member of a team of experts whose job it is to help increase the popularity of seafood and its consumption. Make up some slogans and posters for your campaign. In addition to catchy phrases, be sure to include accurate information about the nutritional value of various kinds of seafood. Share the product of your efforts with the class.

# 📖 *Under the High Seas: New Frontiers in Oceanography*

by Margaret Poynter and Donald Collins
New York: Atheneum, 1983. 166p.

---

This book is almost entirely text, with just a few black-and-white photographs and illustrations. It traces the history of oceanography, discoveries made on the sea floor, currents, and tides.

The book begins with a series of stories or legends about strange happenings at sea from ghost ships of early days to strange time warps that are associated with the Bermuda Triangle.

The authors conclude that we may know more about parts of outer space than we do about the oceans and seas of our own planet.

In chapter three, "Parting the Curtain of the Sea," many famous early sailors and voyages are discussed, including Magellan, the voyage of the *Beagle*, and the *H.M.S. Challenger*.

Chapter five deals with the geological and biological history of our planet as revealed in the late 1960s through the cores that were brought up by the *Glomar Challenger*, an oceanic research ship that sent probes to drill deep in the ocean floor and bring up samples.

Other sections of the book discuss tides and waves; the teeming life of the sea; deep-sea mining, including sand and gravel from shallow coastal waters; oil rigs; power plants; and pollution that is threatening seas and beaches. The final section is a discussion of how people and nations might work together to manage the wealth of the seas.

## Possible Topics for Further Student Investigation

1 Chapter thirteen of this book opens with a few pages that read like the beginning of a science fiction book. It is the authors' attempt to show what might happen in the future if people and nations cannot find ways of working together to share the wealth and the responsibility of healthy seas. With this as your starting point, write your own science fiction short story in which pollution and arguments over the seas have led to international conflicts. In your story, is there a peaceful resolution to the conflicts? Or does your story end in destruction?

2 The book contains a reprint from a whaling museum showing an old whaling ship sinking near Cape Horn. Seascapes of all sorts have been popular with artists throughout the ages. If you like to draw, make your own sketch or painting of a whaling ship foundering at sea. Use whichever medium you prefer. Share your artwork with the class. Or, find art books with various sea paintings, select some that you especially like, and bring these in to share with your classmates.

3 This book discusses the early Greek astronomer who reasoned that there is a connection between the ebb and flow of tides and the appearance and disappearance of the moon. Newton's theory of gravity proved that the early astronomers were right. Make charts explaining the moon's gravitational pull, tidal cycles, and the sun's gravitational pull. Use these charts to explain high and low tides to your classmates.

---

# 📖*Water World*

by Mary Lee Settle
New York: E. P. Dutton, 1984. 120p.

This book is mostly text, with some black-and-white photographs. It traces the history of humans' understanding of the sea from earliest times to modern-day oceanography.

The book begins with an introduction to the vastness of the oceans that cover our planet. It discusses early humans and what they gradually learned as they explored their world by swimming and sailing in the seas. It also presents some of the early legends and stories about gods and strange sea monsters.

Chapter four gives a detailed account of the work of Matthew Fontaine Maury, who, in 1855, published his book about what he had learned of currents and winds, along with his first map of the ocean floor.

The chapter goes on to discuss the invention of the telegraph by Samuel Morse and the attempts of the Atlantic Telegraph Company to lay an underwater cable to carry messages from the United States to Europe.

Chapter seven gives an introduction to both snorkeling and scuba diving. Chapter eight discusses the ocean depths. Following is a chapter on Project Famous, which involved the use of three submersible ships (French and American) to explore the Mid-Ridge Valley off the Azores in 1974. The final portions of the book discuss the rich meadows of the sea, a food chain that does not involve sunlight, and diving for ancient treasures.

## Possible Topics for Further Student Investigation

**1** Mention the word *meadow* and most people will think of a lovely, level spot of land filled with grasses and wildflowers. But the meadows of the sea are quite different. Plankton consists of seaweed and animals. Some fields of plankton have seasons of spring surge, summer ripening, full fall bloom, and winter rest. One of these meadows of plankton is in the Surges Sea. Find out more about plankton. On a map of the world, show your classmates where the Surges Sea is and tell them about the meadows of plankton that are found there.

**2** Diving equipment has changed drastically over the years. Find pictures showing the earliest diving "suits" used by humans and the most sophisticated modern equipment. Include both manned and unmanned means of water exploration. Photocopy the pictures you find and display them with short, informative captions on a class bulletin board that traces the history of diving.

**3** Sometimes ocean currents can be tracked because they are more or less saline than the waters around them. The following experiment will help you show your classmates how salinity affects water currents. You will need: a large, wide-mouthed jar; two glasses; tap water; red food coloring; salt; and blue ink.

Fill each of the two glasses halfway with tap water. Add a drop of red food coloring to one, along with half-a-teaspoon of salt, and stir. Add a drop of blue ink to the other glass, along with three teaspoons of salt, and stir. Then pour the red liquid into the jar. Slowly add the blue liquid. Observe. Do they mix easily? Which goes to the bottom? What do you see several hours later?

# 📖 *Waves, Tides and Currents*

by Daniel Rogers
New York: Bookwright Press, 1991. 32p.

This is a short, easy-to-read book, illustrated with lots of color photographs. It provides a simple introduction to waves, tides, and currents and is part of a series of books about various aspects of the sea.

The first section of this book is devoted to waves. There is a discussion of wind waves, the power of waves, erosion caused by waves, and the ways in which waves create land when pebbles and sand are deposited along a shoreline. One chapter is devoted to tsunamis, which are waves caused by sudden disturbances of the ocean floor. Some of the more famous tsunamis are discussed in detail.

The middle section of the book deals with tidal systems, tidal ranges, and the ways in which the power of tides can be used to generate electricity. It also mentions flooding and ways that people have tried to control coastal flooding.

The concluding section of the book gives information about currents found throughout the top layers of the world's oceans, and then describes the system of currents that is at work in the deep parts of the oceans. The ways in which ocean currents have an effect on land climates is the subject of chapter twelve. This is followed by a discussion of the ways in which currents carry plants, animals, and the various foods that plants and animals need to survive.

## Possible Topics for Further Student Investigation

**1** Cold currents from the Arctic sometimes carry icebergs quite a distance from the polar regions. These can prove dangerous to shipping. One of the most dramatic real-life adventures in sea history involving an iceberg was the sinking of the *Titanic*. Research and read some stories about ships that struck icebergs. Use your data to provide authenticity for a fictional short story about a ship colliding with an iceberg. The setting will be particularly important. What is it like before the ship strikes the iceberg? When alarms sound, how can you create in writing the confusion of the disaster? Will your story have a happy or unhappy ending?

**2** You might want to conduct a science experiment so that you can watch waves in an aquarium. Fill an aquarium that is at least twenty-four inches long halfway with water. Tie four small corks to a weight with different lengths of thread so that one floats one inch from the bottom of the aquarium and the others float two inches, three inches, and four inches from the bottom, respectively. Float one small cork on the top. Make waves by pushing the palm of your hand down on the surface of the water. Study each cork. Move your hand more forcibly or gently to increase or decrease the size of the waves. Tape a ruler to the outside of the aquarium. Draw lines on the side of the aquarium to show the water level and height of the cork on top of the water during a wave.

**3** What kinds of waves are needed for surfboarding? What factors produce these waves? What locations are famous for good surfing? Share what you learn.

# Part IV
# Environmental Concerns

# Environmental Concerns

## ◆ Literature Books ◆

📖*Changes in Latitude*
A family vacation to Mexico ends up being an expedition to save the sea turtle

📖*The Hostage*
A captured whale means big money—until the Save the Whales group gets involved

📖*My Sister Sif*
Erika's adventures with a whale in the South Seas

## ◆ Bridge ◆

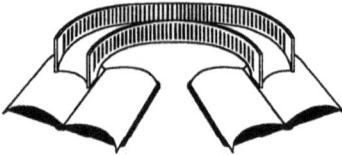

📖*Free Willy*
The popular movie of the rescue and release of a killer whale

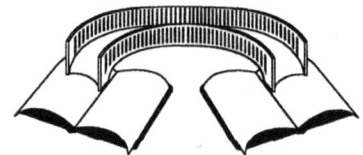

## ◆ Nonfiction Connections ◆

📖*Oil Spill*
The disaster of the *Exxon Valdez* and other oil tankers

📖*Rain of Troubles, the Science and Politics of Acid Rain*
The title tells it best

📖*Saving Our Wetlands and Their Wildlife*
There's much to think about, and it's probably close by

📖*Toxic Waste*
Cleaning up is a big job

📖*The Waste Crisis*
What we throw away, how it affects us, and what can be done

📖*Waste Disposal and Recycling*
Round and round it goes

### OTHER TOPICS TO EXPLORE

—Water treatment plants
—Pesticides
—Fertilizers
—Izaak Walton League
—Environmental organizations
—Impact studies

—Endangered species
—Water diversion
—State fishing regulations
—Federal fishing regulations
—Industrial waste
—Extinction

—Environmental Progection Agency
—Sedimentation
—Erosion
—Army Corps of Engineers
—Effects of dams
—International fishing agreements

# 📖 *Literature Books* 📖

## Environmental Concerns

---

### ◆ Literature Books ◆

📖*Changes in Latitude*
A family vacation to Mexico ends up being an expedition to save the sea turtle

📖*The Hostage*
A captured whale means big money—until the Save the Whales group gets involved

📖*My Sister Sif*
Erika's adventures with a whale in the South Seas

---

### ◆ Bridge ◆

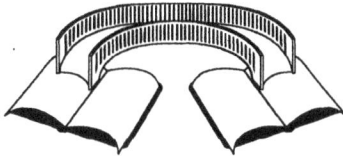

📖*Free Willy*
The popular movie of the rescue and release of a killer whale

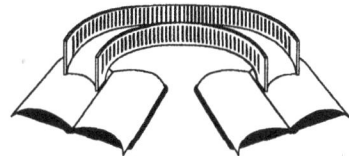

---

### ◆ Nonfiction Connections ◆

📖*Oil Spill*
The disaster of the *Exxon Valdez* and other oil tankers

📖*Rain of Troubles, the Science and Politics of Acid Rain*
The title tells it best

📖*Saving Our Wetlands and Their Wildlife*
There's much to think about, and it's probably close by

📖*Toxic Waste*
Cleaning up is a big job

📖*The Waste Crisis*
What we throw away, how it affects us, and what can be done

📖*Waste Disposal and Recycling*
Round and round it goes

#### OTHER TOPICS TO EXPLORE

—Water treatment plants
—Pesticides
—Fertilizers
—Izaak Walton League
—Environmental organizations
—Impact studies

—Endangered species
—Water diversion
—State fishing regulations
—Federal fishing regulations
—Industrial waste
—Extinction

—Environmental Progection Agency
—Sedimentation
—Erosion
—Army Corps of Engineers
—Effects of dams
—International fishing agreements

# 📖 *Changes in Latitude*

by Will Hobbs

New York: Atheneum, 1988. 162p.

**Type of Book:**
This is a contemporary, realistic book told in the first person from the point of view of a teen-aged boy named Travis.

**Setting:**
Mexico.

**Major Characters:**
Travis, a teen-aged boy; his brother, Teddy, age nine; a sister, Jennifer, age fourteen; his father, Dan, a junior high school science teacher; and his mother, Linda, a pretty woman who'd like to have more money and position and be able to travel like a jet-setter.

**Other Books by the Author:**
*Beardance* (New York: Atheneum, 1993), *Bearstone* (New York: Atheneum, 1989), *The Big Wander* (New York: Atheneum, 1992), and *Downriver* (New York: Atheneum, 1991).

## —PLOT SUMMARY—

The story opens in the airport. Travis is about to fly on vacation to Punta Blanca, Mexico, with his mother, his sister Jennifer, and his brother, Teddy. His father is staying behind. While waiting for their flight to board, their attention is drawn to a display case with information about endangered animals.

As parting gifts, Travis's father gives Travis a tape and Jennifer and Teddy each a book. As Teddy reads on the plane, he learns about a nesting beach of the Pacific ridley a few miles from Punta Blanca, and asks if they can go there and see these sea turtles. His mother responds, "Let's wait until we get there."

Travis is amazed by the taxi ride from the airport to Punta Blanca, saying there isn't an amusement park ride to compare with it. They pass the fancy hotels before arriving at the Sol-Mar, a good choice for the budget-minded. They learn that, even though they have reservations, there are no rooms available. Bill, a young man in the lobby who works for Punta Tours, suggests bribing the desk clerk with $20. It works.

After unpacking, they all try to make the best of their vacation. The young people settle on the beach while Travis's mother, responding to a note she's received, goes off alone. She says she has to take care of something with Aero Mexico concerning the return airline tickets.

The family goes shopping and are impressed with the fruits, baked goods, and souvenirs in the shops. Teddy asks about turtles, and a shopkeeper shows him a stuffed one. Teddy, a young environmentalist, wants to see the live turtles. He discourages customers from buying lotions made from turtles and is disappointed when Travis buys a souvenir that was once a live bullfrog.

To win his way back into the family's good graces, Travis promises to help Teddy find the turtles' nesting spots. Travis learns that Playa Tortugas (Turtle's Beach) is only a short bus ride away.

After getting something to eat and drink, they go down on the beach and soon find a sluggish sea turtle. It is a Pacific ridley. Far down the beach, they discover hatchlings that are headed for the sea. Travis and Teddy chase off the birds and watch the tiny turtles set out into the sea.

They also come upon a man who picks up twenty of the small turtles. He shows them a business card stating that he works at the Laboratorio Salazar. Teddy would like to investigate, but Travis reminds him that it's time to go back to the hotel.

Before they go out that night for a fiesta, Jennifer shares with Travis her fear that their mother will divorce their father. Travis suggests that his mother is just being melodramatic and that Jennifer is blowing things out of proportion. The fiesta ends on a sour note when, against Teddy's protests, they stay to watch a cock fight.

That night, Teddy sneaks out of the hotel room and walks way down the beach to try to see turtles laying eggs. He succeeds in seeing two and in meeting an American marine biologist named Casey, who is also worried about poachers who are stealing eggs. Sneaking back into his room, Teddy wakes Travis, who tells him to go back to bed and get some sleep.

The next morning, Travis looks at girls on the beach. Then he sees a girl, Melissa, falling out of the sky underneath a para-sail. Melissa suggests he try it, and Travis can't refuse. When he gets back, Melissa is talking to Jennifer and Teddy. Travis talks with Melissa while Jennifer tries para-sailing.

That afternoon, while the rest of the family shops, Travis checks out all the hotel lobbies and pools. He meets a parrot who constantly says, "Why not?"

The next morning, Travis hopes to see Melissa again, but he doesn't. When he returns to the hotel, his mother is gone and Jennifer is talking with Bill, the young man they met the day they first arrived. Teddy is reading a book.

Teddy and Jennifer stay where they are, but Travis heads out for Hermosa Beach, where "all the beautiful people go." He stumbles across his mother who is there with Mitch, a man she has been sneaking away to see. Travis overhears her talking about getting custody of Teddy and Jennifer after a divorce and saying that Travis would want to stay with his father.

Travis goes back and gets Teddy and takes him off to look for sea turtles, leaving Jennifer to reconnect with her mother when she returns. Travis and Teddy bump into Casey, who invites them to go out in a boat to locate some turtles.

They find turtles, and Casey gives the boys snorkeling gear and flippers to dive and swim with them. For the first time, Travis feels awe and understands his brother's love for these creatures which are "birds of the sea."

Casey explains that one of the reasons poachers dig up the turtle eggs is that they are believed to be an aphrodisiac. When they part, back at the beach, Travis asks about the schooling necessary to be a marine biologist, and Teddy is wildly happy that his brother is even considering such an option.

Travis and Teddy walk down the beach to the Laboratorio Salazar, which is locked up. They smell something and decide to investigate. They come upon a spot where the birds are eating the carcasses of sea turtles. Near another building they come upon a flatbed truck loaded with live sea turtles.

They go back to Casey to try to get an explanation. He explains that nesting turtles are protected, but that Mr. Salazar has influential friends. The Bureau of Fisheries has given him a variance. There are hundreds of female turtles in an enclosure at the beach whose fate has not yet been decided.

At the Laboratorio Salazar, the eggs from the female turtles that are being slaughtered are supposedly being hatched. They meet Mr. Salazar and are invited to attend the grand opening of his laboratory.

When they get back, they all go out to eat at a fancy restaurant known as Margarita Manny's. Travis manages to provoke a scene at the table, his mother bursts into tears, and they leave. Back at their hotel, they receive a telephone call from Travis's father. The children each talk briefly, and then Travis listens as his mother talks to his father. He hears her say there's only a one or two percent chance she'll not get a divorce.

Both Travis and Teddy wake very early the next morning. The souvenir frog, from which Travis has torn an arm, seems to be staring at them. They walk back to Turtle's Beach and talk about Teddy's dream of swimming and being a turtle, guided by the stars.

Later, Travis sets out to explore the beach on his own, leaving the rest of his family together. He comes upon a thirty-year-old divorcee. They strike up a conversation, and he invites himself to go see her at the Oceano Hacienda that night.

Travis's mother gives them money and takes them to the market for one last shopping trip before the end of their vacation. They look around, eat bananas and *cacahuates* (peanuts), and come upon a beautiful ironwood carving of a sea turtle, which Travis buys for Teddy. Teddy spends his money buying turtle eggs to save them from a group of men who are making drinks out of them.

Back at the hotel, Travis's mother says she's not feeling well and won't go with them to the grand opening of the Laboratorio Salazar. Travis takes one of the turtle eggs, thinking he might need to eat it before his meeting with the divorcee at the hotel.

That afternoon, Jennifer and Travis accompany Teddy to the beach, where he buries his cache of sea turtle eggs. They go through the grand opening ceremony. Travis and Teddy suspect there are no turtle eggs there waiting to be hatched. Instead, there are a few hatchlings that one of the employees has picked up on the beach and taken to the laboratory for show.

Travis gets ready for his date. Before he goes, he drinks the contents of the turtle egg he's saved from those that Teddy bought. Then he tells his sister that their mother is with Mitch. Teddy disappears, but Travis tells his sister to look for him because Travis has a date.

Travis gets to the Oceano Hacienda and goes to the room of the divorcee. She has hurt her neck, so Travis offers to rub it. He finds she has bought turtle lotion. Feeling guilty, Travis runs out of the room and hurries to look for his brother.

Back at the hotel, Travis finds Jennifer. Her blouse is ripped. She took up Bill on his offer of help to go find her brother; instead he ripped her blouse. Jennifer ran away and came back to the hotel. Their mother is still not home.

Travis leaves Jennifer at the hotel and goes to try to find his brother. As Travis looks for Teddy, he remembers things from their childhood, like pretending to rub Teddy's ears to get them warm enough so he could fly.

When Travis finds Teddy, he is dead, and is being held in Casey's arms. Vainly, Travis tries to resuscitate him. Casey says that he found Teddy face down with a sea turtle pinned beneath him. He was apparently trying to free the turtles from the turtle stockade when something happened.

While Travis stays with the body, Casey goes back to the lab to phone the police. He discovers that a window was left unlatched and that Teddy had probably gone back inside, seen no eggs in the hatching sand, released the hatchlings, and then come to carry the turtles from the stockade to the sea.

The police come and so do Jennifer and Travis's mother. She is screaming and crying and has a deep cut in her forehead. At the hospital, Jennifer calls her father to tell him what has happened. He says he'll come at once. Back at their room, Travis tears the rest of his souvenir frog apart and throws it away. He can hear his mother and sister weeping in the next room.

The next afternoon, the family, including Travis's father, go to the morgue to get the autopsy report and to bring clothes for Teddy. Travis brings the carved sea turtle with him and notes that this time the taxi ride is very slow.

They turn over Teddy's clothes and realize then that they brought no shoes for him. They learn that Teddy died of an aneurysm, caused by a weakness since birth and set off by carrying the heavy turtles, which caused a rise in his blood pressure. The family views the body, and Travis puts the carved turtle in Teddy's hands.

While his father makes arrangements to fly the body home, Travis slips out and briefly considers taking his own life. Then he goes back to their hotel, hoping to live for both himself and his brother. His mother has disappeared. His father is looking for her, but Jennifer says no one knows where to look.

Travis goes to the Sheraton Hotel, finds out which room is Mitch's, and goes up to find his mother alone there weeping. She tells Travis that she broke off her affair with Mitch, and they were on their way back to town when they had an accident. That's when she cut her head. Mitch has already left.

Travis and his mother return to the family, where they hope to find forgiveness. Before Travis leaves, he makes one more trip to Playa Tortugas, says a prayer over Teddy's turtle eggs, and, one by one, frees the remainder of the turtles in the stockade.

## 📖 Discussion Starters 📖

*Changes in Latitude*
by Will Hobbs

**1** One thread in the story involves a concern for endangered species that actually starts in the airport before the trip begins and ends when Teddy dies trying to help save the sea turtles. When you read the opening pages of the book, did you suspect that these turtles would play a major part in the story? Why or why not?

**2** At first it seems this is an ordinary family, with Dad seeing the others off on a trip while he stays home because of business or other commitments, but there are several clues in chapter one suggesting that there is trouble in the family. What are these clues?

**3** When Travis takes off, he imagines what his vacation will be like. He has been going over scenarios in his mind where he meets a beautiful stranger. His vacation doesn't end up like his expectations. Have you ever gone on a trip with a notion of how it would be and found it to be something quite different? Was reality better or worse? What was your image of such a vacation, before you took that vacation? What was it *really* like?

**4** Travis's father gives him a cassette tape as a going-away present. He finds the lyrics of a song fits his situation. Many people find popular music "speaks to them." Have you ever found yourself in a situation when a song seemed to fit exactly? What was it?

**5** Travis talks about stereotypes: French are sexy, Russians are warlike, and so on. Have you ever had a stereotype about a person in a particular job, a certain kind of athlete or scholar, someone who lives in a different part of the world, or someone who attends a different kind of school, and then met an individual who proved the stereotype wrong? Describe such as experience, both your stereotype and the reality.

**6** There are situations in this story where the local lotion made from the sea turtle plays a role. Find the various sections where this lotion is mentioned. What function in the story does the lotion play?

**7** Travis is fascinated by the word *cacahuates*, which is Spanish for "peanuts." He says it is "evocative" and the choicest word in the Spanish language. Do you know a word from another language that you think is particularly evocative? What is it and why do you think it is such a great word?

**8** There are many stories where a brother and sister love each other and have conflicts. This is the case between Travis and Jennifer. From your own experience and observation, and from what you have read in other books, do you think the relationship between Travis and Jennifer rings true? Would you change anything in the story to strengthen it?

**9** Travis swallows the contents of a turtle's egg. He does so with a sense of betrayal and says that, during a lifetime, everyone will get the chance to betray someone they love. Knowing the relationship between Travis and Teddy, and knowing the situation each is in, do you think it is logical that Travis eats the egg? Why or why not? What function does this betrayal have in the story?

**10** Jennifer rides off with Bill, with whom she's friendly. Travis goes off to meet the woman from the beach. Teddy's father has refused to make the trip. Teddy's mother is out with another man. If even one of Teddy's family had started looking for him right away, he might have been found before he'd carried so many turtles, and before the aneurysm occurred. Do none, some, or all of the family share responsibility for Teddy's death?

# 📖 **Multidisciplinary Activities** 📖

## *Changes in Latitude*
### by Will Hobbs

**1** A major portion of this book focuses on the Pacific Ridley turtle and the dangers that beset turtle eggs. Do some library research. Locate different places in the world where specific sea turtles come up on the beach to lay their eggs. Use a map of the world to make an oral presentation to your class about what you learn.

**2** The title of this book is *Changes in Latitude*. What do you know about latitude? Our earth is spherical, and beams of light from the sun strike various parts of the earth at different angles at the same moment. Make a model to demonstrate how sunlight strikes the earth differently at different latitudes. (A plastic globe of the earth with balls of clay pressed onto the globe to hold sticks in place so that they cast shadows when a light is turned on them would be one way to show this.)

**3** In this book, turtles are called "birds of the sea." But the properties of air and water are quite different from one another. Devise a number of simple experiments to demonstrate to your class the differences between water and air. You might, for example, use balloons filled with water and with air. What is the difference in weight? Is it easier to change the shape of the water-filled balloon or the air-filled balloon? What happens when you try to submerge the balloons in water? Which is easier to push and hold beneath the surface? What happens to each balloon if you prick it with a pin?

---

# 📖 *The Hostage*

by Theodore Taylor
New York: Delacorte Press, 1987. 160p.

---

**Type of Book:**
This is a contemporary story told in the first person by a fourteen-year-old Canadian boy, Jamie Tidd. It contains considerable factual information about sea creatures, and the author thanks Dr. Marilyn T. Dahlheim of the National Marine Mammal Laboratory in Seattle, Washington, for her assistance.

**Setting:**
The northern Pacific Ocean, near Vancouver, British Columbia.

**Major Characters:**
Jamie Tidd, a fourteen-year-old Canadian boy; his mother, Lace; his father, Papa, or Percy Tidd; and his friend, Angela, age fifteen.

**Other Books by the Author:**
Theodore Taylor's most famous book is *The Cay* (New York: Doubleday, 1969). He wrote a sequel to that book, *Timothy of the Cay* (New York: Harcourt Brace, 1993). Other books include *Air Raid—Pearl Harbor! The Story of December 7, 1941* (New York: Harcourt Brace Jovanovich, 1991) and *The Children's War* (New York: Doubleday, 1971).

## —PLOT SUMMARY—

The story opens in the month of January. Jamie and Papa are on a fishing boat, the *Dawn Girl*, operating out of Lumber Landing in the northern Pacific. Though they had caught only a few fish, the storm forces them to head for home because they must cross eighteen miles of open sea before they reach Hakai Passage.

It begins to snow, and the waves are high and rolling. Papa is alarmed, and both he and Jamie put on water survival suits. A giant wave rolls right over them, but they survive and get home safely out of the storm.

The last fierce storm of the season hits Lumber Landing in April but doesn't stop the mail boat from dumping mailbags, along with two passengers. The mail boat only stops every three weeks because only nine of the eighteen houses in Lumber Landing are now occupied. The cannery was abandoned forty-two years ago. The little town is now home to thirty-two men,

women, and children, and their animals. Five of these families, including Jamie's, are Canadian.

Jamie picks up the Tidds's mail and heads home. Jamie is concerned that among the mail will be a letter from the bank asking for payment of Papa's new boat engine and nets.

The family sits in the kitchen, an especially important room in the Tidd home. Not only is it warm, but it contains fishing gear, a CB radio, and is a place for drying clothes.

Among the mail, Papa reads an advertisement from an ocean park in southern California offering $100,000 in U.S. currency for a blackfish that is twenty-five feet long or longer. "Blackfish" is another name for a killer whale.

Fishermen dislike blackfish because they eat lots of salmon but like them because they eat lots of sea lions (which eat salmon). It is known that the environmentalist group Greenpeace makes it difficult for ocean parks or anyone else to trap whales.

A pod of blackfish always hangs around Queen Charlotte Strait, just north of where the Tidds live and fish. Their boat, the *Dawn Girl*, is used there for trolling and gillnetting.

Jamie's mother, Lace, wants to give up the fishing life for almost anything else. She lost her first husband to the sea when she was only nineteen. Then she met and married another fisherman, Percy Tidd (Papa).

Percy is an independent small-boat operator. He catches spring herring-roe, chinooks, and summer sockeye. He not only likes the sea but likes where his family lives. Among the wildlife in their area are grizzly bears, wolf, wolverine, bald eagles, ospreys, and humpback and killer whales. There are also forests of firs, cedar, spruce, and hemlocks.

For two winters, Jamie has gone to school in Port Hardy at the end of Vancouver Island. But this year there isn't enough money, so he is being schooled through migrant education courses mailed to him every month from Victoria.

In June, Angela Pinheiro comes home after her second year in high school. Angie is fifteen and the only person in the town who is near Jamie's age; all the other children are five or younger. While she goes to school, she stays with relatives. Her mother and father take a float plane to visit her at Christmas. In the summer, Angie works on a boat belonging to her father, Cristo. Her three sisters are married and gone from home. Angie has crewed on the *Funchal* since she was nine.

When Angie comes home, she tells Jamie about the boy she's met, and she tells a wild story about winning $5 for accepting a dare and walking naked around a ledge of a building four stories tall. Angie always makes a point of topping anything Jamie says.

Jamie's grandfather tries to keep the family in touch with the world. He sends Jamie a dirt bike magazine. He also gave the family a TV and a satellite dish.

After a day's fishing, Jamie and Papa catch about $800 worth of big king salmon. They head for the buy-barge in Fitz Hugh Sound. Jamie spies a spout of a humpback whale. They then see three blackfish that swim up and kill and eat the whale.

Jamie goes to Angie's to watch a movie, but her father chases him off. The two teenagers take Angie's skiff to get some supplies at Critchelow. While they are caught in a dense summer fog, they hear the killer whales making whistles, clicks, buzzes, screams, and snorts.

Angie teases Jamie for being afraid. Then Angie doesn't answer Jamie when they land. He starts to worry that she's fallen into the water but finds out she is simply hiding and teasing him again.

The next day, through their binoculars, Papa and Jamie spy the three killer whales at Wilwilli Cove. A whale goes into the cove, and Papa heads for it, planning to drop a couple of nets across the entrance and trap the big whale. They manage to drop three layers of net, catching the killer whale in the cove.

Angie comes to look at the whales. Two smaller ones linger outside the cove. She names them Persephone and Desdemona. Then she begins talking to the big whale that is trapped in the cove. The whale seems to whistle back.

When Doc Greenlee, a veterinarian; Mr. Tebbetts, an animal trainer; and Mr. Cooke arrive, they name the trapped whale Tyrannus. Doc Greenlee has just met Mr. Cooke. Mr. Tebbetts had worked at Sea World, and only recently was hired as an animal trainer at the new, better-paying ocean park.

Doc Greenlee explains how noisy it is underwater. Sound travels four times faster there than in the air, and there are lots of creatures making noise in the water as well as the bumping of the rocks, the sound of boat propellers, and so on.

Jamie has touched Tyrannus and said it was a wonderful experience. The trainer and the doctor are satisfied with the condition of the whale, so they call Mr. Cooke to go ahead with the deal to pay for the whale and move it to the ocean park. Mr. Cooke has developed the photos of the whales that Papa took earlier, and he wants exclusive rights to them.

The men from the ocean park plan to build a sea pen out of steel bars and oil drums about sixty feet long and forty feet wide, with a catwalk around the top. Then they plan to come back and tow the whale to Vancouver. The final part of the plan is to charter an Air Canada freighter to quickly transport the whale in a sheepskin hammock to Los Angeles.

After the visitors leave, Papa's photos of the whales are shown on television. Angie runs over to tell them. Jamie goes to find his father and sends him home to watch the ten o'clock news while Angie and Jamie stay to watch Tyrannus.

The next day a helicopter arrives from BC News to film a program about the whale. This program portrays Jamie and Papa as greedy fishermen who are holding the killer whale as a hostage. Doc Greenlee calls to warn them that animal rights activists everywhere are up in arms and might even send pickets to the cove.

Leaving Jamie to watch the whale, Papa goes to buy salmon for Tyrannus. Jamie falls asleep, and Angie comes to the cove. By this time, she seems to be almost under the spell of the whale. She put on a survival suit to keep warm and jumps into the water. Tyrannus catches her by the arm, pulls her to the bottom, and keeps her there.

Jamie grabs a salmon and jumps in, too. He releases the salmon and Tyrannus swims after it. Jamie is then able to pull Angie to the surface and administer CPR. Then he runs for help. A helicopter airlifts Angie and her father to Port Hardy.

A call comes from Doc Greenlee saying that the deal to sell the whale to the ocean park is off. The Save the Whales group has caused so much trouble that the park owners have decided to give up on the idea. All Papa got from his efforts was $500 for the pictures he'd taken.

Papa and Jamie take in their nets, and the whales leave. A call to the hospital lets them know that Angie is doing fine and also allows them to share with her the news that the killer whale is free.

A few days later, Angie comes home. Jamie tells her that he loves her both for what she's done and for who she is.

# 📖 Discussion Starters 📖

*The Hostage*
by Theodore Taylor

**1** This story begins with a storm at sea that almost sinks Jamie and Papa. Why do you think the author chose to begin the book with a storm?

**2** What do you think is the significance of the fact that Jamie's grandfather, who lives in California, sends him a subscription to *Dirt Riders*, a dirt bike magazine?

**3** Angie's father worries about her and warns Jamie not to touch her. Why does Jamie think that he is in more danger from Angie than Angie is from him?

**4** Jamie has fished all his life. Why, then, do tears spring to his eyes when he and his father see the humpback attacked by the killer whales? What insights into Jamie's character do you get from this episode?

**5** In chapter nine, Angie pretends briefly to be dead by resting against a burial stone in a tiny cemetery just south of Little Norway. What reason do you think the author had for including this scene in the book?

**6** As soon as they trap the killer whale in the cove, Jamie feels he's "doing something wrong." He knows this is not a fish for eating but a mammal. Does it make sense to you that it's all right to catch and eat big fish from the sea but not all right to catch sea mammals? Why or why not?

**7** When Angie first sees the blackfish, she immediately thinks it should be freed. Angie says it's an "insult" to put an animal like this in an ocean park and teach it to perform tricks. Do you agree or disagree? Why?

**8** The men name the blackfish Tyrannus. Angie thinks that Willy would be a better name. Which name do you prefer? Why? Can you come up with a better name than either of these?

**9** When Jamie and Papa see themselves on the television program about Tyrannus, they are very disappointed. The program has been rigged to make them look greedy. Can you think of instances when newspapers or television news shows may have been deliberately slanted to give one particular view of an event? Describe what happened.

**10** Even though they have lost their dream of wealth, Lace manages to make Papa laugh, and Papa hugs his son and wife and says, "We'll survive." Why did the author interject humor at this point in the story?

From *Bridges to the World of Water*. © 1995. Teacher Ideas Press. (800) 237-6124.

## 📖 **Multidisciplinary Activities** 📖

### *The Hostage*
### by Theodore Taylor

**1** Jamie and his father catch salmon. Research this variety of fish. In what waters do most of the salmon live? How many kinds of salmon are there? Is one kind more plentiful than another? Which kinds of salmon are used for food? Is most salmon sold to consumers fresh, frozen, or canned? Is salmon a popular fish in the United States? In what countries is the consumption of fish per capita higher than in the United States? Once you have your data, prepare some graphs and share them with your class.

**2** A conservationist group that is mentioned in the story is Greenpeace. When was this group formed? What is its purpose? In what ways have its members been active? Some people are opposed to this group. Find factual information about Greenpeace and its activities. With classmates, prepare a debate in which two people defend the merits of Greenpeace and two people expose any problems resulting from the group's activities.

**3** Fishing is a very dangerous occupation. Many laws have been passed requiring that certain equipment, including survival suits, be kept on board fishing boats. Investigate and find out what the laws are that regulate commercial fishing. Prepare a written report on what you learn. Be sure to cite your sources of information.

## 📖 *My Sister Sif*

by Ruth Park
New York: Viking Penguin, 1991. 180p.

**Type of Book:**
   This book is a fantasy, told in the first person by Erika, who was fourteen when these events occurred.

**Setting:**
   Rongo Island, southwest of Tahiti.

**Major Characters:**
   Fourteen-year-old Erika; her sisters, Sif and Joanne; her island friends, Pig, Mummy Ti, and Dockie; Erika's underwater family members, who are seapeople; and a young marine scientist, Henry.

**Other Books by the Author:**
   *Playing Beatie Bow* (New York: Atheneum, 1982), *Road Under the Sea* (Garden City, N.Y.: Doubleday, 1965), and *Things in Corners* (New York: Viking, 1989).

### —PLOT SUMMARY—

When Erika's father, Erik Magnus, died, Joanne became the guardian of her two younger sisters, Erika and Sif. Joanne has two children of her own, Giselle, age two, and Travis, age six.

Years earlier, Erik Magnus, a Scandinavian seaman, jumped ship and swam to Rongo Island, southwest of Tahiti. The Polynesians welcomed him, and he married a girl called Matira. The only other white man on the island was Dockie, who had served as a medical officer, taught the children, and opened a general store with Erik Magnus.

When they got older, the three children were sent to boarding school in Sydney. Joanne would spend the holidays with her school friends, but Erika and Sif always came back to Rongo Island.

Sif wants to be back on Rongo Island this year in June when the whales come. Erika suggests that they run away to Rongo Island. To finance their trip, they'll sell shells they had collected on the island. That won't be enough money, so Erika suggests that Sif go first, borrow from Dockie

the additional money that Erika will need, and mail it to her.

While Erika is selling the shells, she meets an eager customer in the shop. Erika buys a plane ticket for Sif, and Sif leaves on a plane the next morning. Erika pretends to be ignorant about Sif's trip when questioned by Joanne. Travis has seen Erika say good-bye to Sif, but he doesn't tell.

The day that Erika leaves the city, Travis is waiting to see her off and asks her to tell his Grandma about him. Erika forgets to leave behind the note she wrote to Joanne.

When Erika flies to join Sif, she ends up on the same plane with Henry Jacka, the customer she met in the shell shop. He has learned about the Epiphany Islands and is on his way there. He works for the Friedlander Museum.

Dockie and Mummy Ti meet Erika. They all live in what used to be Erika's father's house behind the store. Mr. Jacka shows up again just as Erika's brother,

*113*

Stig, appears. Mr. Jacka can't believe his eyes because he sees that Stig is a merman.

Erika's mother, Matira, a mermaid, appears. She is glad to see Ricorico, which is Erika's real name and means "dancing sparkle on creek water." Matira returned to her seapeople when Erika was only four, leaving her to be raised by her father and Dockie.

Erika tells her mother how her grandson, Travis, was born with webbed hands and how he has dark eyes. Erika makes plans with her brother, Stig, to visit the undersea city the next day. The others refuse to worry about Henry Jacka discovering their secrets. They know that the islanders will discount any story he tells.

The next morning, when Erika is on the bottom of the lagoon, Henry Jacka, thinking Erika is drowning, tries to save her. He tells her that he has decided to move here from the big island to do his diving. Sif surfaces and is introduced to Henry.

When Henry comes to the store and asks about mermen and merwomen, Dockie says that of course he believes in them and in menehune, the tiny people who built the breakwater and jetty and who live underground up in the hills. When the missionary, Mr. Spry, comes in the store and confirms this story, Henry stomps off, thinking they're teasing him.

That afternoon Sif and Erika go to meet Stig. Sif can swim underwater far longer than Erika, who uses a rebreather, a device that seapeople use on long trips. As Erika is playing with the dolphins, she sees Henry watching them with binoculars.

Thinking that Sif and Erika are drowning, Henry swims out to save them, and then runs barefoot across the coral to Dockie's. Mummy Ti bandages his feet and suggests that Dockie tell Henry the truth. When Sif and Erika get home, Erika realizes that Henry loves Sif and will try to take Sif from her.

Erika decides to have a menehune help her to drive Henry away. She runs up into the mountains, where she meets Father Axe and rubs noses with him. Father Axe talks to Pig about driving Henry away. Pig wears jeans and has punk-rock

hair. He is one of the "rare" menehune, in that he wants to join the people of the human world. Together they plot some mischief to drive Henry away. Erika agrees to pay Pig with a radio and a box of caramels.

Later when Erika sees Sif, she apologizes to Mummy Ti and to Henry for being rude the night before. She goes to see a sea creature, Emere, and learns that her baby dolphin was deformed and has died. The other dolphins come and tell a sad story of oil slicks and poisons in the sea. They want Erika to do something about the pollution.

Erika goes to talk to Dockie, but he is angry because he's just received a letter from Joanne and knows now that Erika did not leave a note for her but just disappeared. Joanne is angry and writes that Erika can't come back to finish school and go to the university to study to become a marine biologist.

Erika goes to find Sif, but Sif is out in a boat with Henry, so Erika goes to her secret place where there is an old statue. Pig comes along and tells Erika that he loves her and wants to marry her when they grow up. Erika tells Pig that she only wants to be friends and that she can't live in a burrow.

Erika hears some noises and fears that Pig has done mischief without waiting for her signal. She's right. Henry is tied up in the swamp, and his cottage is in ruins. Erika steals Henry's yellow notebook and finds Pig. Using Pig's knife, Erika frees Henry. When they come out of the swamp, they find Mummy Ti and others looking for them. Henry takes everything in stride and says two boys played a trick on him.

While Erika is swimming, she gets a message that a baby whale is about to be born and that's why the dolphins aren't around. Erika swims out deeper and goes too far. A shark comes, and Erika must stay very still, although she is almost out of breath. An "aunt" whale comes and helps her, and then calls the dolphin to take her in the shallow water to the beach.

For a couple of days, Erika is in bed and delirious. Dockie tells Henry the truth about the merpeople, and Erika tells Dockie how badly the waters are polluted. But Dockie says there is nothing he can do about it.

Erika returns Henry's notebook and writes a letter of apology to Joanne. She knows that Sif and Henry are falling in love but realizes there is nothing she can do about it.

Erika visits the missionary and sees the new bathroom that the menehune are making for him. She is ashamed of the way she treated Pig. That night, Henry comes to dinner and learns that he will get to visit the underwater city the next day. After dinner, Erika goes back to the missionary's to see Pig and set things right with him. The rest run away, but Pig comes to her and takes her to a beautiful underground cave.

Pig then tells her that all the seapeople are going away to a place called Kopu. The sea has become polluted from atomic experiments and the water is poisoned. The next morning, Erika faces Dockie and asks why he hadn't told them the seapeople were leaving. He admits his cowardice and suggests that Sif may leave, too. When Erika tells Sif that the seapeople are leaving, Sif runs off to her mother.

Stig shows Henry around and tries to explain why they must leave. He says that since the 1980s, when industrial nations began burrowing down into the ocean floor from Hawaii to Samoa to mine for cobalt and manganese, huge cracks began appearing. Poisonous gas has squeezed out and killed vegetation.

Stig goes to his sister, Sif, while Erika shows Henry around. Henry asks about the light, *te mata*, which isn't the result of electricity. Erika then tells Henry everything about the seapeople.

When Stig comes back, Erika goes to her mother, Matira, who is demanding that Sif come away with her. Erika does what she can to insist that Sif make up her own mind. They go to the wall of the city and find many humpback whales making a huge sound.

They return to Mummy Ti, and Sif is very weak. Dockie says she must stay in bed and makes plans to take her to the big island for X-rays because he doesn't like her persistent cough.

Henry stays away while Sif makes up her mind whether to go or stay. Mummy Ti says she will give Matira bad dreams. Sif is not strong enough to go back to the city, so the seapeople come in to say good-bye. Matira is subdued and says Sif must stay.

Erika goes up into the mountains and sees the menehune. Pig battles another menehune named Mud, and Mud wins the right to marry a rare female menehune.

Sif, Henry, and Erika go to say good-bye to the sea city. While they are there, the island volcano rumbles and the city collapses. Henry is caught in the debris. Sif gives him her rebreather and goes to get help from an islander.

Erika cuts Henry free with Pig's knife, which she always carries. The islander comes and dives down and helps free Henry, but Sif is lost. It is presumed that she did not take a deep enough breath and has drowned.

After all this tragedy, Joanne takes Erika back into her home. Later Erika goes to college. Henry returns and begins working actively to try to save the seas from pollution. Erika writes to Henry's brother, Martin.

Erika goes to Kopu hoping to find the seapeople, but instead finds it almost deserted. An old islander, carving a seaman, tells Erika that the seapeople came but left again. Martin joins Erika there, and they work together to save endangered species. Joanne's two children come and work with them, too.

Now that she's older, it's hard, but Erika manages to "talk" with a whale who tells her that the seapeople are now at Meru. Erika never finds this place, which may be heaven or a place that is hidden on earth beneath the seas.

Mummy Ti has gone back to her own island after Dockie's death, but Erika and Martin go back to Rongo Island, where they visit the menehune and see Pig. Pig believes that things are improving on Rongo Island and throughout the world. On this positive note, the book ends.

# 📖 Discussion Starters 📖

*My Sister Sif*
by Ruth Park

**1** When did you first suspect that Erika and Sif were not completely normal people but were part of a fantastical family of mermaids and mermen? What clues led you to suspect that something was unusual about them?

**2** Not only does this book have a world of seapeople, it has a world of tiny people, the menehune, who live on land. The story of the menehune is not essential to the telling of the story about the seapeople. Why do you think the author created both worlds? Is the book stronger because of the inclusion of the menehune?

**3** Three people play the part of "mother" to Erika in this book: Mummy Ti, Joanne, and Matira. Each sees the role of mother differently. How are these three alike and how are they different in the role of mother?

**4** Pig is shown to be different from other menehune in that he likes many of the things of the human world and even professes loving Erika and wanting to marry her when they are old enough. Why do you think Pig is different than the other menehune? At the end of the book, do you think Pig is content with his lot?

**5** At first, Erika is jealous of Henry. What are the things that Henry does and says that eventually win Erika's affection?

**6** Joanne, Sif, and Erika are sisters. In what ways are they alike, and in what ways are they very different?

**7** There are many ways in which the author could have shown the results of pollution in the sea. She chose to use a dead baby whale and a deformed baby porpoise. Why do you think these symbols were chosen? Were they effective?

**8** If partway through the book you were told that either Sif or Erika would die before the book ended, would you have guessed that Sif would be the one to die? What clues were given by the author that might have led you to reach this conclusion?

**9** It is suggested that, as Erika grew older, it became more difficult for her to communicate with whales and dolphins. What do you think might account for this?

**10** It is unclear from the book whether the seapeople have all died or whether they have moved to another kingdom beneath the sea. Which do you think is the case? What supports your opinion?

# 📖 Multidisciplinary Activities 📖

*My Sister Sif*
by Ruth Park

**1** Erika and Sif plan to get the money for their plane fare by selling valuable shells. Research shells. What kinds of shells are most valuable to collectors? What do such shells look like? What makes them so valuable? Bring in pictures of some of these shells to share with the class. If you know someone who has a shell collection, invite that person to come and share information about seashells.

**2** Erika can communicate with the seapeople. Many experiments have been conducted by scientists trying to learn more about dolphin communication. Learn what you can about this intriguing area of research. Where has the research taken place? Was it successful? What have scientists learned about the ways in which dolphins communicate? Share what you learn with the class.

**3** Erika's brother suggests that much of the pollution in the sea has been caused by mining for cobalt and manganese. For what purposes are cobalt and manganese used? Where are they abundant? How are they mined? From what you learn, determine whether or not Erika's brother's belief about the cause of ocean pollution is correct. Share your work with the class.

From *Bridges to the World of Water.* © 1995. Teacher Ideas Press. (800) 237-6124.

# 📖 *Bridge* 📖

## Environmental Concerns

---

### ◆ Literature Books ◆

📖*Changes in Latitude*
A family vacation to Mexico ends up being an expedition to save the sea turtle

📖*The Hostage*
A captured whale means big money—until the Save the Whales group gets involved

📖*My Sister Sif*
Erika's adventures with a whale in the South Seas

---

### ◆ Bridge ◆

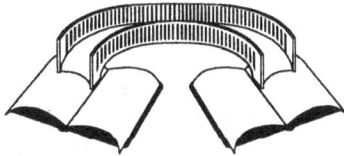

📖*Free Willy*
The popular movie of the rescue and release of a killer whale

---

### ◆ Nonfiction Connections ◆

📖*Oil Spill*
The disaster of the *Exxon Valdez* and other oil tankers

📖*Rain of Troubles, the Science and Politics of Acid Rain*
The title tells it best

📖*Saving Our Wetlands and Their Wildlife*
There's much to think about, and it's probably close by

📖*Toxic Waste*
Cleaning up is a big job

📖*The Waste Crisis*
What we throw away, how it affects us, and what can be done

📖*Waste Disposal and Recycling*
Round and round it goes

#### OTHER TOPICS TO EXPLORE

—Water treatment plants
—Pesticides
—Fertilizers
—Izaak Walton League
—Environmental organizations
—Impact studies

—Endangered species
—Water diversion
—State fishing regulations
—Federal fishing regulations
—Industrial waste
—Extinction

—Environmental Progection Agency
—Sedimentation
—Erosion
—Army Corps of Engineers
—Effects of dams
—International fishing agreements

# 📖*Free Willy*
Burbank, Calif.: Warner Brothers, 1993. 122min.

This popular movie, made available on video in late 1993, describes the conflicts that arise and the friendships that develop when a young boy becomes part of a training team preparing a captive whale, Willy, for a marine park type of show.

The boy, who has been abandoned by his mother, becomes involved in criminal mischief and is placed with foster parents.

As he struggles to understand how to trust others and to become part of a family, he is especially sensitive to Willy's need to be reunited with his family in the sea.

When Willy fails to perform, his owner decides to drain the water in Willy's pool to kill the whale and then collect on his insurance. This leads Willy's friends to undertake a daring rescue and release.

## Possible Topics for Further Student Investigation

**1** So that he will perform successfully in a show, Willy is trained. Professional animal trainers work in a number of different fields. Some train animals for programs similar to Willy's at various marine parks. Others may train animals to perform in circuses, in movies, or in television shows. Still others teach dog obedience courses or train guide dogs for the visually impaired. In your area, locate an animal trainer and invite him or her to visit your class and discuss how successful training of animals is achieved.

**2** There are many different types of whales. Study the different types, locate pictures or make sketches of the various types, and display these on a bulletin board. Beneath each type, be sure to include such information as where it is found, how big it is, and what it eats.

**3** One of the phrases used in the film is a sort of chant that repeats the word *S'gana*. In your library, locate and read the book *S'gana, the Black Whale* by Sue Stauffacher (Anchorage: Northwest Books, 1992), and share with your class an oral report about the book. The book, like the film, involves a distressed whale at a local marine park.

# 📖 *Nonfiction Connections* 📖

## Environmental Concerns

### ◆ Literature Books ◆

📖*Changes in Latitude*
A family vacation to Mexico ends up being an expedition to save the sea turtle

📖*The Hostage*
A captured whale means big money—until the Save the Whales group gets involved

📖*My Sister Sif*
Erika's adventures with a whale in the South Seas

### ◆ Bridge ◆

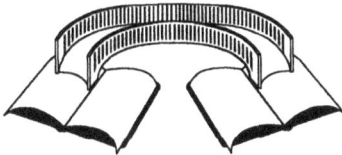

📖*Free Willy*
The popular movie of the rescue and release of a killer whale

### ◆ Nonfiction Connections ◆

📖*Oil Spill*
The disaster of the *Exxon Valdez* and other oil tankers

📖*Rain of Troubles, the Science and Politics of Acid Rain*
The title tells it best

📖*Saving Our Wetlands and Their Wildlife*
There's much to think about, and it's probably close by

📖*Toxic Waste*
Cleaning up is a big job

📖*The Waste Crisis*
What we throw away, how it affects us, and what can be done

📖*Waste Disposal and Recycling*
Round and round it goes

#### OTHER TOPICS TO EXPLORE

—Water treatment plants
—Pesticides
—Fertilizers
—Izaak Walton League
—Environmental organizations
—Impact studies

—Endangered species
—Water diversion
—State fishing regulations
—Federal fishing regulations
—Industrial waste
—Extinction

—Environmental Progection Agency
—Sedimentation
—Erosion
—Army Corps of Engineers
—Effects of dams
—International fishing agreements

# 📖 *Oil Spill*

by Christopher Lampton
Brookfield, Conn.: Millbrook Press, 1992. 49p.

This is a short, easy-to-read book that is illustrated with color photographs. It chronicles the story of the disaster that resulted when the oil tanker *Exxon Valdez*, in attempting to avoid icebergs in Prince William Sound in March 1989, hit a reef and caused a gigantic oil spill.

The oil spill caused by the *Exxon Valdez* was one of the most widely publicized in modern times. Eleven million gallons of oil poured into the Sound, spoiling beaches and killing wildlife. The attempts to clean up after this oil spill went on for years, and there is debate as to how successful these efforts were.

Lampton devotes several sections of his book to a discussion of where oil comes from, how the petroleum industry has grown in the United States, and how oil makes the world go round. He documents its importance and shows the many ways that it has been transported throughout history.

Other sections of the book detail the largest oil spills of all time, including Ixtoc I and the Persian Gulf spills, which did not involve tankers, and the aftermath of these various spills on waters, beaches, and wildlife.

The final chapter of the book suggests that, through a search for alternative forms of energy generation, we can cut down on the amount of oil that we use, transport, and spill.

## Possible Topics for Further Student Investigation

1. When people feel strongly about a topic, they often share those feelings through editorials and letters to the editor in newspapers and magazines. Or they may write to a senator or a congressperson and urge political action. Another way of sharing a political view is through a political cartoon. If you were a political cartoonist during the time of the *Exxon Valdez* oil spill, what image would you use to convey your opinions about this disaster to the public? Draw several cartoons and share them with your class. Survey your classmates to see which cartoon is most effective and why.

2. This book contains a simple map that shows oil-field areas, major oil-producing regions, major oil consumers, and the locations of nineteen major oil spills dating back to 1957. Prepare a similar map for a bulletin board and share it with your class. You will have to do some additional research to make it as up-to-date as you can.

3. Lampton points out that some of the worst damage resulting from oil spills is the damage to the food chain. If oil kills plankton, which live in the water, then the animals that depend upon the plankton for food die. In turn, the animals that depend upon plankton-eating animals die, and so on. Research this topic. Then prepare a presentation on food chains, using diagrams or pictures, and share it with your classmates.

# 📖 *Rain of Troubles, the Science and Politics of Acid Rain*

by Laurence Pringle
New York: Macmillan, 1988. 122p.

This book contains mostly text with a few black-and-white photographs and charts. It provides a thoughtful and critical look at water supplies and water management. This book has won several honors, including selection as a "Best Book of the Year" by the *School Library Journal* and an "Outstanding Science Trade Book for Children."

The book documents several incidents of destruction attributed to acid rain, including trout that died in Norway's Torvdal River and the loss of half of the spruce trees on Camel's Hump in the Green Mountains of Vermont.

The author explains how acid rain is formed, how it is transported, and how it affects life on both water and land throughout the world. He discusses how acid rain can be controlled through the latest technology and how economics and politics affect the decision-making process that could result in a reduction of the poison, through acid deposition, which can fall as rain or as dry particles.

Chapters one through four provide a factual presentation of what has been learned about acid deposition and the ways it is formed and transported. The last two chapters of the book suggest how acid rain can be controlled and what economic and political forces are at work in the United States on both sides of this issue.

## Possible Topics for Further Student Investigation

1  In any discussion of acid rain, you need to understand that the term *pH* stands for "potential hydrogen" and is a measure of the number of positively charged hydrogen ions concentrated in a substance. The pH scale ranges from 0 to 14, with 7 indicating a neutral substance, less than 7 indicating an acidic substance, and greater than 7 indicating an alkaline substance. Unpolluted rainwater is slightly acidic. Find out more about pH. Learn about and perform some simple tests to show the pH of a variety of common liquids. Graph your results and share them with the class.

2  In the mid 1970s, the United States and Canada set up long-term programs to study the chemistry of precipitation. Find reports about the acidity of precipitation in the United States from different years. Use transparencies of a map of the United States projected on your classroom wall to share with fellow students information about which parts of the United States have a precipitation pH of less than 4.2 or more than 5.5.

3  Chapter six of this book discusses the politics of acid rain. It tells about numerous newspaper accounts and articles that appeared in a variety of magazines discussing the problem over the past fifteen years. It also outlines steps taken by the presidential administration of President Carter to deal with the problem. A major concern in taking action to eliminate acid rain is the economic effect of such an action on regions where high-sulfur coal is mined. With a group of interested students, prepare a panel discussion outlining various ways that might be recommended to deal with the acid rain problem in the United States and Canada.

# 📖 *Saving Our Wetlands and Their Wildlife*

by Karen Liptak
New York: Franklin Watts, 1991. 64p.

This is a small, easy-to-read book illustrated with color photographs. It discusses wetlands, what lives in them, why they are disappearing, and why, in some areas once threatened, wetlands are making a comeback.

The book begins by pointing out that wetlands have value and should be saved. There is a detailed discussion of both freshwater and saltwater wetlands. Various terms are explained: *swamp, marsh, bog, bottom land,* and *prairie pothole.*

The value of wetlands as major breeding grounds for waterfowl, amphibians, and mammals is presented. The value of a wetlands as a water reserve, flood control area, and waste filter are all pointed out, and an explanation is offered as to why wetlands in the United States are endangered.

The book discusses various plants that live in the wetlands, including bald cypress trees, tupelo, pop ash, Spanish moss, spider lilies, cattails, and resurrection ferns. It also points out the birds and animals that live in wetlands, including spoonbills, ibis, snowy egrets, ducks, salamanders, turtles, snakes, alligators, bobcats, otters, and raccoons.

Sections of the book are devoted to various efforts throughout the country to save sections of wetlands. The book concludes with tips on how to dress to safely visit marshy areas.

## Possible Topics for Further Student Investigation

1. Are there any wetland areas near your community? If so, consult with state or local parks and recreation personnel, members of the fish and game division, sportsman's clubs, environmental groups, and so on to identify the wetland closest to you. Arrange for a visit to the wetland with a knowledgeable guide who can explain the importance of wetlands and who can introduce you to the various plants and animals that live there. Take slides of your visit. Present a slide show to the class to share what you have learned.

2. This book mentioned the Whooping Crane Tracking Project and gives its address: Whooping Crane Tracking Project, Project Leader, U.S. Fish and Wildlife Service, 2604 St. Patrick, Suite 7, Grand Island, NE 68803. Write to this agency with questions you may have about the whooping crane. Be sure to include a large, self-addressed envelope with postage. Ask this agency to send any available pamphlets and materials. Using this material, and other information that you find, prepare a classroom bulletin board about whooping cranes.

3. Many bird lovers are especially interested in wetlands, which are essential to many species of bird life. Try to locate a member of the National Audubon Society from your community who is willing to come and visit your class and talk about birds and wetlands. If possible, ask the speaker to bring slides or photographs to share.

# 📖 *Toxic Waste*

by Susan Dudley Gold
New York: Crestwood House, 1990. 48p.

This is a short book, illustrated with color photographs. It is part of a series of books called Earth Alert. It seeks to present the issue of toxic waste in easy-to-understand language with accurate scientific information.

The book begins with a warning from Love Canal, a town in northern New York only six miles from the famous Niagara Falls. The Hooker Chemical & Plastics Corporation had dumped metal drums containing wastes from pesticides into the canal between 1942 and 1953. Then they covered the cans with soil and eventually sold the land to the town for the token sum of $1. A school was built on the land; children attended the school and played in the creeks nearby. After the buried metal drums rusted, the wastes poisoned the area. In 1978, President Carter declared an environmental emergency and arranged for more than 1,000 families to be moved from the area.

The book then explores the subject of toxic waste: what it is and how it moves through the food chain. There are sections on chemical dumps, toxins in the air, pesticides and herbicides, PCBs, waste oil, accidents at nuclear power plants such as Three Mile Island and Chernobyl, and nuclear waste.

Other sections deal with the dangers of transporting wastes on the highways and a variety of household hazards such as asbestos, radon, and household chemicals.

## Possible Topics for Further Student Investigation

1 Your community may already have in place a way of dealing with toxic wastes. For example, your community may have a waste disposal center that designates certain days throughout the year when people may bring in hazardous substances to be disposed of in a responsible and safe manner. Large school districts may also have plans and policies for dealing with toxic wastes, especially from such areas as chemistry and photography labs. Find out where the closest center for toxic waste is in your community. Invite someone from that center or someone who deals with toxic wastes in your school district to visit your class and share information.

2 In certain parts of the country, radon is perceived to be a problem. Why? Radon is a colorless, odorless gas that is formed when radioactive radium decays. Tests are used to find out if there is too much radon gas in homes or schools. One common and inexpensive test involves placing small canisters of material in several locations in a building and then sending the canisters to a laboratory for professional evaluation. The results will show the radon level for each area. Your science teacher may be willing to allow you to test for radon in the science room of your school. Share the results with your class.

3 Contact your state or federal representatives. Ask them to provide you with information about any environmental bills currently before the state legislature or U.S. Congress. Study these bills. If you have an opinion on one or more of them, send a letter stating your position to the appropriate elected official.

# 📖 *The Waste Crisis*

by Jenny Tesar
New York: Facts on File, 1991. 112p.

This is an excellent introduction to the waste crisis facing the world. It is illustrated with both black-and-white and color photographs. Of particular interest to students involved in a unit of study about oceans and seas will be chapters seven and eight, which deal with wastewaters and the treatment of wastewaters.

The first third of the book documents where wastes come from, where they go, and why we are facing a waste crisis. The second third of the book describes hazardous wastes, including radioactive wastes, and how they are handled. The final topics to be considered are wastewaters and the reduction of waste.

Although many books have documented the problems we face in dealing with waste by pointing the finger at major polluters, they often don't provide information about what an ordinary citizen can do to help solve the problem. In this book, steps for reducing waste and various recycling efforts are detailed.

The book lists a number of things from the "good old days" that, in some cases, are being reintroduced in the interest of waste management. These include soft drinks and beer in refillable bottles, fountain pens with refillable ink, cloth diapers, and cloth shopping bags. Information is presented on how some companies are switching packaging so that containers can be refilled, and how newly designed crates can help eliminate the need for cardboard boxes and fillers.

## Possible Topics for Further Student Investigation

1. One problem that we face is that of "junk" mail. Most people receive catalogues and mailings that they do not want and do not request. How big is the junk mail problem? With interested friends, carry out an experiment. In each home involved, use a container to collect junk mail for a two-week period. Weigh the mail at the end of the two weeks. Share the results of your experiment with your classmates.

2. Most of us use batteries in a variety of ways. They power games, toys, flashlights, calculators, and watches, among other things. In many countries of the world, old batteries are recycled instead of discarded. This is not a common practice in the United States. One firm, however, Mercury Refining Company of Latham, New York, has been reclaiming mercury and silver from batteries. Such reclamation can help communities to set up battery recycling programs. Write to this company and find out more about its reclamation efforts. Be sure to include a self-addressed stamped envelope with your request for information. Share what you learn with your classmates.

3. If your school is like most, it already has some recycling efforts under way. But after beginning a recycling effort, people sometimes lose interest and become careless. Use your artistic abilities to heighten awareness, renew interest, and further these recycling efforts. Design posters with catchy slogans to encourage students and staff to recycle. With the permission of your school principal, hang your posters in areas where they might be most effective.

# 📖 *Waste Disposal and Recycling*

## by Sue Becklake
New York: Gloucester Press; Aladdin Books, 1991. 36p.

---

This is an easy-to-read, large-format book illustrated with color photographs. It is part of a series of environmental issues books called Green Issues: Thinking for the Future.

Chapter one points out that as modern life has evolved, sewage, chemical fertilizers, plastics, manufacturing processes that cause pollution, and other factors have led to a tremendous increase in wastes. Other sections in the book deal with our "throwaway society," population growth, and the depletion of our natural resources.

Of particular interest in this unit of study on oceans and rivers is chapter two, which describes how dirty water is one of the world's greatest killers. It details how waste from industries and sewage from homes are regularly disposed of in many parts of the world by piping them into rivers or seas where they spread disease among humans and kill wildlife.

Chapter four explains that when toxic waste is burned at sea, the smoke and gases escape and pollute the air and the water. The ash that is dumped into the ocean causes more pollution.

The final chapter of the book is devoted to describing ways that have been found to reduce industrial waste and to reuse industrial materials and household garbage. Recycling efforts and tips for ordinary citizens to reduce waste are included.

## Possible Topics for Further Student Investigation

1. What sorts of recycling efforts are going on in your school and in your community? Consider whether there might be some special project that your class could undertake to aid in the recycling effort. Are aluminum pop cans from the teachers' lounge being recycled? Is the school cafeteria using a lot of plastic throwaways? Are there recycling waste receptacles in your building for various kinds of scrap paper? If there are areas that could be improved, hold a class discussion. Have interested members of your class plan and carry out a particular recycling effort with the approval of the school administrator.

2. There are many arguments in favor of and in opposition to the use of various pesticides in gardens and on farms. In some parts of the country, use of certain pesticides is forbidden or can only be carried out after notice has been given to people in surrounding areas. Although there are dangers, the use of pesticides greatly increases agricultural production. With a few other interested class members, research the use of pesticides on farms. Find out positive and negative effects of using pesticides. Present a panel discussion on the topic for your classmates.

3. Algal bloom is the rapid growth of tiny water plants that occurs when sewage or fertilizers get into the water and supply too much plant food. Do some library research on this topic, locating at least three sources of information. Write a short paper on the topic and include a bibliography. Share your report with your class.

---

# Part V
# Additional Resources
# and Linkages

# 📖 Questions That Link Various 📖 Fiction Books

For the activities listed below, form small groups based on students who have read both of the books on which the activities are based. There are no right and wrong answers, but opinions that are given should be supported by the text of the books.

**1** In *The Hostage*, Jamie Tidd forms a kinship with a live killer whale after he touches it. Touching the beached whale is important in *You Must Kiss a Whale*. In what ways are the authors' uses of touching the whale in *You Must Kiss a Whale* and in *The Hostage* alike and different?

**2** In *Haunted Journey*, Obie is left with his dead father's debts. In *You Must Kiss a Whale*, Evelyn feels that her father has saddled her with a strange legacy. How are the feelings of Obie and Evelyn about their fathers alike and different?

**3** In *The Blue Heron*, the heron takes on a special significance for Maggie just as Jamie develops a special feeling for the killer whale in *The Hostage*. How are the roles of the heron and the killer whale alike and different?

**4** In *The Blue Heron*, Maggie's father keeps it a secret that he has been fired from his job. In *Haunted Journey*, Obie doesn't tell Bas the truth about the number of pearls he's found. Are these secrets of equal importance? What do you think would have happened in each case if the person with the secret had shared it?

**5** In *The Blue Heron*, Maggie finds it hard to talk to her father about her worries concerning his failure to take his medicine. In *The Hostage*, Jamie can't talk to his father about his experience in touching the blackfish. What are the barriers that prevent these two from communicating with their fathers?

**6** In *You Must Kiss a Whale* and in *The Last Voyage of the Misty Day*, a mother and daughter cope with the loss of their husband/father. In what ways do the two mothers and two daughters behave similarly and in what ways do they react differently to their loss?

**7** In *Haunted Journey* and in *The Last Voyage of the Misty Day*, the central character in the book falls into the water and almost drowns. Is the author's purpose in showing the near drowning the same in each book, or is the purpose different in one book from what it is in the other?

**8** *The Hostage* takes place in a small town in the Northwest; *The Last Voyage of the Misty Day* takes place in a small town in the Northeast. In what ways are Phinney's Island and Lumber Landing alike and different?

**9** In *The Hostage*, the two whales that stay outside the cove are given the names of Persephone and Desdemona. In *The Last Voyage of the Misty Day*, the two engines are given the names of Stella and Penelope. In each case, what did the author achieve by using these names?

**10** The heron in *The Blue Heron* has a special significance for Maggie just as the sea turtles in *Changes in Latitude* have special importance for Teddy. How are the roles of the heron and the sea turtle alike and different?

**11** In *Haunted Journey*, Obie keeps a secret from Bas. He doesn't tell him the truth about the number of pearls he's found. In *Changes in Latitude*, Travis doesn't tell Jennifer about what he's discovered about his mother. Would it have been better in either case, as things turned out, for the person who kept the secret to tell the truth? Why or why not?

**12** In *Changes in Latitude*, Travis takes two taxi rides. In *You Must Kiss a Whale*, Kevin takes a taxi ride. The rides were very different. What was the function of each of the rides in the books?

**13** In *Beyond the Reef*, Chris's mother is disappointed in her husband and keeps leaving him to go back to Flintville. In *Changes in Latitude*, Travis's mother says there's only a small chance that she won't divorce her husband. Do you think either of these marriages will last another ten years? Why or why not?

**14** In *You Must Kiss a Whale*, Evelyn tries to find some of the answers to her concerns about her father by looking through a manuscript she finds in her mother's trunk. In *Beyond the Reef*, Chris tries to find some of the answers to his father's treasure hunting problems by reading an old manuscript written by a seventeen-year-old sailor long ago. How is the function of the manuscript the same and different in each of these stories?

**15** A friendship of several years between a boy and a girl is featured in *Beyond the Reef* and in *The Hostage*. In both cases, the two young people are separated for several months. When they get back together, they notice changes. What are the changes noticed in each book?

**16** In *The Last Voyage of the Misty Day*, Denny suspects Spence of being the person who beat up the captain. In *Dragon of the Lost Sea*, Shimmer thinks she has been betrayed by Thorn when he seems to offer to become Civet's cook to save his own life. As each pair of characters knew each other well, was the suspicion justified? Do you think you would have been equally suspicious under those circumstances? Why or why not?

**17** In *My Sister Sif*, Erika and Sif, who have a mermaid for a mother, are concerned about the destruction of the seapeople and a kingdom beneath the sea. In *Dragon of the Lost Sea*, Shimmer remembers her beautiful city and wants to restore the sea and the kingdom. Conversely, Civet has bitter memories of her life beneath the sea. Compare the descriptions of life beneath the sea in these two books. How are they alike and different?

**18** There is a net of burning mesh that plays an important role in *Dragon of the Lost Sea*. A net also plays a major role in *The Hostage*. Think about the function of the net in each of these stories. How are the nets the same and how are they different?

**19** There is a dragon in *Dragon's Plunder* and a dragon in *Dragon of the Lost Sea*. How are these two dragons alike and how are they different? Which dragon do you like best and why?

**20** How is the relationship between Jamie and Amelia in *Dragon's Plunder* alike and different from the relationship between Jamie and Angela in *The Hostage*?

**21** Mr. Jones in *The Last Voyage of the Misty Day* and Captain Deadmon in *Dragon's Plunder* each are involved in a sort of quest. Each is committed to doing something before being at peace. How are these two "quests" alike and different?

**22** In *Dragon of the Lost Sea* and in *Dragon's Plunder*, a boy who works in an inn leaves it and goes out into the world to seek adventure. In both cases, the boys are orphans. What else do these two boys have in common? How are they different?

**23** In *The Hostage*, Mrs. Tidd has been married to two sailors. She would give almost anything for a life not connected to the sea. In *Dragon's Plunder*, the princess, Amelia, is clearly planning out a future for herself and her young friend in which he would be an admiral in her navy. Do you think that, in a few years, Amelia will feel like Mrs. Tidd? Why or why not?

**24** In *The Last Voyage of the Misty Day*, Denny's mother, at the beginning of the story, has given up writing, but by the end of the book she is writing again. In *Dragon's Plunder*, Mr. Pye has given up writing but has plans to resume by the end of the book. In which book is the writing subplot most important? Why?

**25** In *Beyond the Reef* and in *The Last Voyage of the Misty Day*, a number of people come together to help the boat captain get ready to go to sea. What role does this support from community members play in each book?

**26** Kingdoms beneath the sea are destroyed in both *Dragon of the Lost Sea* and *My Sister Sif*. Both kingdoms are described in considerable detail. Compare the two kingdoms. How are they alike and how are they different?

**27** In *The Blue Heron*, a young stepmother, Joanna, finds herself trying to meet the needs of her husband's child as well as of her own baby. In *My Sister Sif*, Erika's older sister, Joanne, must care for Erika and Sif as well as her own two young children. Both Joanna and Joanne have problems to face with their combined families. How are their problems alike and different?

**28** Monkey is a minor but interesting character in *Dragon of the Lost Sea*. Pig is a minor but interesting character in *My Sister Sif*. How are Monkey and Pig alike and different? Which character do you like best? Why?

**29** A river is actually an important "character" in both Gary Paulsen's *The River* and Ruth Riddell's *Haunted Journey*. In each book, a boy almost drowns but is ultimately given up safe and sound by the river. Compare the events. How are they alike and different?

**30** Brian's mother in *The River* is reluctant to have her son return to the wilderness but is supportive of his decision. Obie needs to sneak away without letting his mother know of his journey and must stand up against her on his return in *Haunted Journey*. Compare the actions of these two mothers. How does their support or lack of it affect the main characters' actions?

**31** Chris saves Shannon's life by using a knife in *Beyond the Reef*. Brian saves Derek's life by using a knife in *The River*. How are these two rescues alike and different? Which was more central to the story? Why?

**32** In *Seaward*, Westerly is jealous of Cally's attraction to the snake and her experiences with him. In *The Hostage*, Jamie is jealous of the boys and experiences that Angela has had while going to school without him. How does this jealousy influence each of the characters?

**33** In *Seaward*, Ryan is a kindly "mother" figure who helps Cally. In *Dragon's Plunder*, Clara Llewellan is a kindly "mother" figure who helps the Princess Amelia. How are Ryan and Clara alike and different? How does each one influence a young girl?

**34** In *The True Confessions of Charlotte Doyle*, Charlotte lives through wild adventures and finds it very difficult to readjust when she returns to her normal surroundings. In *The River*, Brian finds it difficult to adjust to being in the city again after his adventures in the wilderness. Both characters leave their normal surroundings to return to the more adventurous lives they come to know. Why do you think it was so difficult for each to adjust?

**35** In *The Blue Heron*, Maggie is worried that her father will die. In *Seaward*, Cally is worried that her father will die. Is this worry about death more central to one of the stories than the other? Discuss.

**36** In *You Must Kiss a Whale*, Evelyn assumes most of the responsibility for her little brother because her mother is preoccupied and is dealing in bizarre ways with being abandoned by her husband. In *Changes in Latitude*, Jennifer has responsibility for her little brother because her mother is preoccupied with a decision about a divorce. In what ways are these situations similar and in what ways are they different?

**37** In *The Last Voyage of the Misty Day*, Denny, who now is in Maine, misses her old girlfriend back in Brooklyn. In *You Must Kiss a Whale*, Evelyn misses her friend Michelle. Neither of the friends has a major role. What is each friend's function?

**38** Compare Captain Octavius Deadmon from *Dragon's Plunder* with Captain Jaggery in *The True Confessions of Charlotte Doyle*. How are they alike? How are they different?

**39** Denny admires Mr. Jones in *The Last Voyage of the Misty Day*, but Mr. Jones turns out to be someone different from her original image. Charlotte at first admires Captain Jaggery in *The True Confessions of Charlotte Doyle*, but he turns out to be different from her first impressions. Examine the changes in feelings of the two girls toward the two captains. How are the changes alike and different?

**40** In *Changes in Latitude*, it is the younger brother, Teddy, who, it seems to his older brother, Travis, has many insights. In *Stormsearch*, Tim comes to realize that his little sister, Tracey, is very insightful. What sorts of insights does Teddy have? Are they similar or different from those that Tracey has? Why do you think the author gave such insights to the youngest characters in the two books?

**41** In *Stormsearch*, Tim feels that his parents are so caught up in their third-world activities that they do not devote enough time to him and his needs. In *Beyond the Reef*, much of the time, Chris feels abandoned by his mother and ignored by his father who is lost in his own treasure-hunting world. Do you think that Tim and Chris were really abandoned? How would each set of parents defend themselves against such a charge?

**42** There is a story within a story in both *You Must Kiss a Whale* and *Stormsearch*. Do these stories within stories serve the same purpose? What is the purpose of each and how do they differ in plot function from one another?

**43** There is a beached whale in both *Why the Whales Came* and *You Must Kiss a Whale*. Each of these whales is a symbol having to do with how people treat one another and fellow creatures. Discuss the symbolism of the whale in each story.

**44** In *Beyond the Reef* and in *Why the Whales Came*, young people borrow a boat, have an adventure, and cause others to worry for their safety. Compare the reception that Chris got when he was found to be safe with the reception that Daniel and Gracie received from their parents. Did all the parental reactions seem valid? Why do you think the parents reacted differently?

**45** There is a carving of a dragon in *Seaward*, a carving of a turtle in *Changes in Latitude*, and a carving of a cormorant in *Why the Whales Came*. Each carving had a role to play in the plot. Choose any two of these books. Which carving do you think was most important to its overall story and why?

# 📖 Additional Individual 📖 Projects

## Arts

**1** One often hears, "You can't judge a book by its cover," but covers are important to books. When a student has finished reading a book, ask the student to study its cover. Have the student consider whether or not the cover is a good choice for the book. Ask the student to design a new book jacket and be able to explain why the new art is more appropriate.

**2** There are very few illustrations in chapter books written for young adults. Encourage those students who like to draw to choose a particular scene from a fiction book they enjoyed and to illustrate it. Have others who have read the book comment on the illustration.

**3** Present the following scenario: Suppose that one of the fiction books that you especially like was going to be made into a movie and you were given the task of selecting a piece of music that would be played as the titles and screen credits appeared on the screen. What piece of music would you select for which book? Share a little of the music with your class and explain why you think it is particularly fitting for the book you selected.

## Speaking/Listening/Critical Thinking

**1** Often a book has a key phrase or paragraph that captures the essence of the entire book. Have a student select such a phrase or paragraph and read it to the class, explaining why he or she thinks this particular section of the book is so important.

**2** In many fiction books there is a clash of values. Sometimes the clash occurs between those who would make an economic profit and those who would be strict conservationists. Sometimes the clash is between generations. Have each student choose one of these conflicts that interests them. Have students select from the book a section that illustrates the conflict, read it to the class, then try to explain both sides of the conflict.

## Reading/Writing/Research

**1** When a student has finished a fiction book, ask the student to write a short review of the book, including whether or not the student would recommend it to others and why. These book reviews can be saved in a collection so that when students are selecting a fiction book, they can refer to reviews written by other students.

**2** For the student who likes to write, suggest that he or she choose a place in the book where another short chapter might be inserted. Ask the student to write the chapter. Then, with others who have read the book, have the student share the new chapter and explain why it was inserted into the book at this place.

**3** Nonfiction writing will appeal to some students. Have a student choose a topic relating to oceans, rivers, and seas and research that topic. Ask the student to write an article between 600 and 1,200 words on the topic and to include a list of all sources of information used to prepare the article.

**4** A book may lend itself to research. For instance, in *Haunted Journey*, the subject of the Great Depression comes up. If student interest is triggered by something in one of the fiction books, encourage further research on the topic of interest and help the student find a means in small- or large-group activities to share what he or she learns.

**5** Sometimes it seems that characters in books are named at random. Other times it seems that the name is chosen to in some way comment on the character. Have students choose a couple of the names from fiction books that they think have particular meaning, then write a short paragraph on each name explaining how they think the name added meaning to the book.

# 📖 Additional Small-Group 📖 Projects

## Arts

**1** Every reader has a favorite section of dialogue from a book. Have a student choose a section of dialogue that is particularly important to the book. Have that student cast classmates to play roles in the dialogue and direct them to convey the emotion that seems appropriate. When ready, have the students present these small scenes before the class.

**2** Lots of music has been written about the sea. There are even recordings of whales and other sea creatures and tapes with the sounds of water to listen to while falling asleep. Have a group of interested students listen to some of this music, perhaps with the help of a music teacher, and discuss among themselves what it is that makes it "water music."

**3** A small group of students might create a mural to capture the main themes that emerge from one of the fiction books. Have students design the mural, choose a medium in which to work, then complete the mural and share it on a class bulletin board. Engage the rest of the class in small-group discussions about the mural.

## Speaking/Listening/Critical Thinking

**1** If there is a group of students interested in poetry, ask them to select some poems that have some relationship to oceans, rivers, seas, or the birds and animals we associate with these areas. Have students read the poems to the class.

**2** Several of the fiction books in this volume are fantasy. Have a small group interested in this genre gather together, then give them one character and a name such as "Lyndar the Dragon." Have them form a circle and make up a fantasy, with each student adding to the adventure. (You might want to tape-record this for future reference.)

## Reading/Writing/Research

**1** Take one of the fiction books that a small group of students have all read. Ask each group member to share with the group some other fiction book not on the list that came to mind because of some similarity in plot, character, setting, and so on.

**2** Have a small group of interested students write a nonfiction picture book on animals of the ocean or animals of rivers to share with a primary-grade class. Do research to be sure that the material prepared is accurate. Have the group edit and critique the manuscript to be sure that the text is lively. Set the text with a typewriter or computer. Have one or more members of the group illustrate the book. Select a member to read it to a primary-grade class and report on its reception.

# 📖 Additional Large-Group 📖 Projects

## Arts

**1** Because all the core fiction books and the nonfiction books in this volume relate to oceans, rivers, and seas, dedicate a wall of the classroom to a class mural. Form committees to plan the mural and assign tasks.

## Speaking/Listening/Critical Thinking

**1** Book titles are important. Have students discuss the titles of several of the core books. Ask questions such as: Why do you think a particular title was selected? Is the title appropriate? If you were to retitle one of these books, what new title would you choose? Why?

**2** Stories are held together by tensions. These tensions hold our interest by making us anxious or holding us in suspense. Ask students to think back on a fiction book that they have read. Have them list of few of the "tensions" that exist in the story. List these on the chalkboard. Then ask students to identify what they believe to be the major or central tension in a book. Create lists for other books. Have students compare the lists of tensions. How are they alike?

## Reading/Writing/Research

**1** For each of the fiction books in this volume, put up a chart that lists the main characters. Ask students to write words on the chart that are used to describe the characters. As the lists grow, take some time to compare the various lists.

**2** Most books will contain unusual words or words new to students. Ask students to jot down unfamiliar words that they find while reading the core books in this volume. List these words and their definitions. Discuss what purpose the author may have had for choosing these particular words.

**3** Writing is often referred to as "hands-on thinking," and for this reason many teachers like to ask their students to keep a reading log. In addition to noting the title and author of the books being read, students are encouraged to write comments, either at times that seem appropraite to them or at certain times specified by the teacher, related to setting, mood, style, and so on.

**4** Reading and writing times should go together. During the class reading time, be sure to allow time for writing and drawing, or both. Have students jot down thoughts about characters, moods, and incidents, or sketch images of settings they have formed from reading. Hold teacher/student conferences to talk about the story the student is reading and his or her written or artistic reactions to it.

## 📖 Ideas for Using Picture Books with 📖 Middle-Level Students

There are many beautiful fiction and nonfiction picture books that might be used for a variety of purposes in a middle-level classroom. The examples that follow are just a few ideas to get you started.

**1** Relate a simple picture book to a more difficult young adult fiction book. *Dragon's Plunder* is a young adult book. During the course of the story, the sailors need a magical wind for their ship, there is an attack by a pirate ship, and a dragon comes to the rescue. *Cyrus the Unsinkable Sea Serpent* by Bill Peet (Boston: Houghton Mifflin, 1975) is a picture book. In it, there is also a magical wind, an attack by a pirate ship, and a dragon that comes to the rescue. Ask interested students to compare these two books and to discuss the relationships of similar plots and characters.

**2** *The River* describes a wilderness experience in Canada where a boy relies upon a river to bring an injured man to civilization. *Paddle to the Sea* by Holling Clancy Holling (Boston: Houghton Mifflin, 1941) also deals with a craft, a river, and the Canadian wilderness. Have students compare these books.

**3** *The Mysteries of Harris Burdick* by Chris Van Allsburg (Boston: Houghton Mifflin, 1984) employs a series of strange drawings. Some of these relate to oceans, rivers, and seas. Ask students to look at one of the following pictures from the book and to write an original short story inspired by the picture: *Captain Tory*, *The Harp*, *Missing in Venice*, or *A Strange Day in July*.

**4** Several of the fantasies in the fiction books include dragons. Ask students to study the drawings in *Saint George and the Dragon*, retold by Margaret Hodges and illustrated by Trina Schart Hyman (Boston: Little, Brown, 1984). After studying these pictures, and the pictures from the young adult fantasies, ask students to demonstrate their appreciation of the various art styles.

**5** Several of the young adult fiction books deal with whales and with carvings. An exploration of cultural diversity and an understanding of analogous concepts might emerge from a discussion of these fiction books along with the picture book *Whale Brother* by Barbara Steiner (New York: Walker, 1988).

**6** Some young adult books contain fantasy and some have elements of mystery. Use the following picture books to teach models for these two literary genres: *Winter Whale* by Joane Ryder (New York: Morrow Junior Books, 1991) and *The Wreck of the Zephyr* by Chris Van Allsburg (Boston: Houghton Mifflin, 1983). What are the elements of fantasy and mystery in each book and how does each author use these elements?

## 📖 Additional Fiction Titles 📖

*Amy's Eyes*, by Richard Kennedy. New York: Harper & Row, 1985. 437p.

*Boat Song*, by Frances Ward Weller. New York: Macmillan, 1987. 168p.

*The Changeling Sea*, by Patricia A. McKillip. New York: Atheneum, 1988. 137p.

*I Sailed with Columbus*, by Miriam Schlein. New York; HarperCollins, 1991. 136p.

*Island of the Blue Dolphins*, by Scott O'Dell. Boston: Houghton Mifflin, 1990. 181p.

*The Mermaid Summer,* by Mollie Hunter. New York: Harper & Row, 1988. 118p.

*Neptune Rising, Songs & Tales of the Undersea Folk*, by Jane Yolen. New York: Philomel, 1982. 149p.

*Sarah and Me and the Lady from the Sea*, by Patricia Beatty. New York: Morrow Junior Books, 1989. 182p.

*Seventeen Against the Dealer*, by Cynthia Voigt. New York: Atheneum, 1989. 181p.

*S'gana, The Black Whale*, by Sue Stauffacher. Anchorage: Alaska Northwest Books, 1992. 221p.

*Shadow Shark*, by Colin Thiele. New York: Harper & Row, 1985. 214p.

*A Stranger Came Ashore*, by Mollie Hunter. New York: Harper & Row, 1975. 163p.

*Water Sky*, by Jean Craighead George. New York: Harper & Row, 1987. 212p.

*Whalesinger*, by Welwyn Wilton Katz. New York: Dell, 1990. 212p.

*Windcatcher*, by Avi Wortis. New York: Bradbury Press, 1991. 124p.

## 📖 Additional Nonfiction Titles 📖

### Ships, Diving, and Treasure

*Archaeology Under Water: An Atlas of the World's Submerged Sites*, edited by Keith Muckelroy. New York: McGraw-Hill, 1980. 192p.

*Cousteau: An Unauthorized Biography*, by Axel Madsen. New York: Beaufort Books, 1986. 270p.

*The Discovery of the Titanic*, by Robert D. Ballard. New York: Warner Books, 1987. 230p.

*Dive to Adventure*, by Jack McKenney. Vancouver, British Columbia, Canada: Panorama, 1983. 144p.

*Down Under, Down Under: Diving Adventures on the Great Barrier Reef*, by Ann McGovern. New York: Macmillan, 1989. 48p.

*The Explorers of the Undersea World*, by Richard Gaines. New York: Chelsea House, 1994. 111p.

*Exploring the Deep Frontier*, by Sylvia Earle and Al Giddings. Washington, D.C.: National Geographic Society, 1980. 296p.

*Exploring the Titanic*, by Robert D. Ballard. New York: Scholastic, 1990. 64p.

*Gold & Silver, Silver & Gold: Tales of Hidden Treasure*, by Alvin Schwartz. New York: Farrar, Straus & Giroux, 1988. 128p.

*Hidden Treasures of the Sea*, by the National Geographic Society. Washington, D.C.: National Geographic Society, 1988. 104p.

*Sea Disasters*, by Rhoda Nottridge. New York: Thomson Learning, 1993. 48p.

*Treasure Hunt: The Sixteen Year Search for the Lost Treasure Ship, Antocha,* by George Sullivan. New York: Henry Holt, 1987. 150p.

*Sunken Treasure*, by Gail Gibbons. New York: Thomas Y. Crowell, 1988. 32p.

*Titanic*, by Frank Sloan. New York: Franklin Watts, 1987. 95p.

*Titanic: Triumph and Tragedy*, by John P. Eaton and Charles A. Haas. New York: W. W. Norton, 1986. 319p.

*Treasures of the Deep*, by Walter Olesky. New York: Julian Messner, 1984. 189p.

*Undersea Archaeology*, by Christopher Lampton. New York: Franklin Watts, 1988. 96p.

*Underwater Dig: The Excavation of a Revolutionary War Privateer*, by Barbara Ford and David C. Switzer. New York: William Morrow, 1982. 154p.

*Unlocking Secrets of the Unknown*, by the editors of the National Geographic Society. Washington, D.C.: National Geographic Society, 1993. 200p.

## Animals and Plants Living in and Around the Sea

*America's Seashore Wonderlands*, by the Special Publications Division of the National Geographic Society. Washington, D.C.: National Geographic Society, 1985. 200p.

*The Atlantic Gray Whale*, by Jan Mell. New York: Crestwood House, 1989. 48p.

*Between Cattails*, by Terry Tempest Williams. New York: Charles Scribner's Sons, 1985. 28p.

*Discovering Seashells*, by Douglas Florian. New York: Charles Scribner's Sons, 1986. 30p.

*Great White Shark*, by Richard Ellis and John E. McCosken. New York: HarperCollins, 1991. 270p.

*Homes in the Sea: From the Shore to the Deep*, by Jean Sibbald. Minneapolis, Minn.: Dillon Press, 1986. 95p.

*How Did We Find out About Life in the Deep Sea?* by Isaac Asimov. New York: Walker, 1981. 61p.

*Humpback Whale*, by Michael Bright. New York: Gloucester Press, 1990. 32p.

*Inside the Whale and Other Animals*, by Steve Parker. New York: Doubleday Books for Young Readers, 1992. 47p.

*Life in a Tidal Pool*, by Alvin and Virginia Silverstein. Boston: Little, Brown, 1990. 60p.

*Life in the Sea*, by Jennifer Coldrey. New York: Bookwright Press, 1991. 32p.

*Monsters of the Deep*, by Norman S. Barrett. New York: Franklin Watts, 1991. 32p.

*Monsters of the Sea*, by Rita Golden Gelman. Boston: Little, Brown, 1990. 32p.

*The Night Lives On*, by Walter Lord. New York: William Morrow, 1986. 272p.

*Ocean Life*, by Les Holliday. New York: Crescent Books, 1991. 62p.

*Ocean World*, by Tony Rice. Brookfield, Conn.: Millbrook Press, 1991. 64p.

*An Octopus Is Amazing*, by Patricia Lauber. New York: Thomas Y. Crowell, 1990. 32p.

*Pond & River*, by Steve Parker. New York: Alfred A. Knopf, 1988. 63p.

*Seasons of the Cranes*, by Peter and Connie Roop. New York: Walker, 1989. 28p.

*Sharks, the Super Fish*, by Helen Roney Sattler. New York: Lothrop, Lee & Shepard, 1986. 96p.

*The Whooping Crane, a Comeback Story*, by Dorothy Hinshaw Patent. New York: Clarion Books, 1988. 88p.

*Wonders of the Sea*, by Louis Sabin. Mahwah, N.J.: Troll, 1982. 32p.

# Understanding, Exploring, and Surviving

*Exploring the Sea: Oceanography Today*, by Carvel Blair. New York: Random House, 1986. 96p.

*New Lands, New Men: America and the Second Great Age of Discovery*, by William H. Goetsmann. New York: Viking, 1986. 528p.

*The Ocean Floor*, by Keith Lye. New York: Bookwright Press, 1991. 32p.

*Oceanography—Science Frontiers*, by Martyn Bramwell. New York: Hamstead Press, 1989. 45p.

*Oceans*, by Philip Whitfield. New York: Viking, 1991. 72p.

*Our Amazing Ocean*, by David Adler. Mahwah, N.J.: Troll, 1983. 31p.

*Principles of Underwater Sound*, by Robert J. Urick. New York: McGraw-Hill, 1983. 423p.

*Restless Oceans*, by A. B. Whipple. Alexandria, Va.: Time Life, 1989. 176p.

*Rivers, Ponds and Lakes*, by Anita Ganeri. New York: Dillon Press, 1991. 45p.

*Under the Sea*, rev. ed., by Brian Williams. New York: Random House, 1989. 24p.

*A Walk on the Great Barrier Reef*, by Caroline Arnold. Minneapolis, Minn.: Carolrhoda Books, 1988. 47p.

*Walking the Wetlands*, by Janet Lyons and Sandra Jordan. New York: John Wiley, 1989. 222p.

*Water World*, by Mary Lee Settle. New York: Lodestar Books, 1984. 120p.

*The World's Oceans*, by Cass R. Sandak. New York: Franklin Watts, 1987. 32p.

# Environnmental Concerns

*Acid Rain*, by Robert Boyle and Alexander R. Boyle. New York: Schocken Books, 1983. 146p.

*Acid Rain: A Plague upon the Waters*, by Robert Ostmann. Minneapolis, Minn.: Dillon Press, 1982. 208p.

*Caring for Our Water*, by Carol Greene. Hillside, N.J.: Enslow, 1991. 32p.

*Coral Reefs in Danger*, by Christopher Lampton. Brookfield, Conn.: Millbrook Press, 1992. 63p.

*Endangered Species,* by Christopher Lampton. New York: Franklin Watts, 1988. 128p.

*The Global Ecology Handbook,* by Walter H. Corson. New York: Global Tomorrow Coalition, 1990. 414p.

*Hazardous Substances, a Reference,* by Melvin Berger. Hillside, N.J.: Enslow, 1986. 128p.

*Oceans in Peril,* by John C. Fine. New York: Macmillan, 1987. 141p.

*Oceans of the World: Our Essential Resource,* by Kirk Polking. New York: Putnam, 1983. 112p.

*Polluting the Oceans,* by Michael Bright. New York: Gloucester Press, 1991. 32p.

*Pollution and Wildlife,* by Michael Bright. New York: Gloucester Press, 1987. 32p.

*Toxic Chemicals, Health, and the Environment,* by Lester B. Lave and Arthur C. Upton. Baltimore, Md.: Johns Hopkins University Press, 1987. 304p.

*Toxic Threat: How Hazardous Substances Poison Our Lives,* by Stephen J. Zipko. New York: Julian Messner, 1986. 193p.

*Troubled Skies, Troubled Waters: The Story of Acid Rain,* by Jon Luoma. New York: Viking, 1984. 178p.

## 📖 Selected Magazines 📖

*Calypso Log*

*Dive Industry News*

*Diver*

*Diving & Snorkeling*

*The Dry Dock*

*Dolphin Log*

*Environmental Science & Technology*

*National Geographic*

*Natural History*

*Ocean Realm*

*Scuba Times*

*Sea Frontiers*

*Skin Diver*

# 📖 Selected Videos 📖

*Africa's Stolen River*, National Geographic Society.

*Alaska: Outrage at Valdez*, Turner Home Entertainment.

*Atocha: Quest for Treasure*, National Geographic Society.

*Bering Sea: Twilight of the Alaskan Hunter*, Turner Home Entertainment.

*Captains Courageous*, Metro-Goldwyn-Mayer.

*Ducks Under Siege*, National Audubon Society.

*Free Willy*, Warner Brothers.

*The Great Whales*, National Geographic Society.

*Haiti: Waters of Sorrow*, Turner Home Entertainment.

*Himalayan River Run*, National Geographic Society.

*Iceland River Challenge*, National Geographic Society.

*Jaws*, Universal Pictures.

*Moby Dick*, Moulin Productions.

*National Geographic NOVA Special,* "Great White Shark," National Geographic Society.

*Papua New Guinea: The Center of Fire*, Turner Home Entertainment.

*Search for the Battleship Bismark*, National Geographic Society.

*Secrets of the Titanic*, National Geographic Society.

*The Sharks*, National Geographic Society.

*20,000 Leagues Under the Sea*, Walt Disney Productions.

*Western Australia: Out West Down Under*, Turner Home Entertainment.

# Author-Title Index

# *About the Author*

Dr. Phyllis J. Perry has taught in California, New Jersey, and Colorado, from second grade to graduate school. She has been a teacher, a curriculum specialist, a director of talented-and-gifted education, a principal, and a university supervisor of student teachers. Throughout, she has had a strong interest in a multidisciplinary approach to education.

Dr. Perry is the author of nineteen books for children and adults, including *A Teacher's Science Companion* (TAB Books/McGraw-Hill, 1994), *Colorado History* (Hi Willow Press, 1994), and *Getting Started in Science Fairs* (TAB Books/McGraw-Hill, 1995). She also writes plays, poetry, articles, and fiction for a variety of children's magazines.